NINE INDIAN WOMEN POETS

NINE INDIAN
WOMEN POETS
An Anthology

Edited by

EUNICE DE SOUZA

DELHI
OXFORD UNIVERSITY PRESS
CALCUTTA   CHENNAI   MUMBAI
1997

Oxford University Press, Great Clarendon Street, Oxford OX2 6DP

Oxford New York
Athens Auckland Bangkok Calcutta
Cape Town Chennai Dar es Salaam Delhi
Florence Hong Kong Istanbul Karachi
Kuala Lumpur Madrid Melbourne Mexico City
Mumbai Nairobi Paris Singapore
Taipei Tokyo Toronto

and associates in

Berlin Ibadan

ISBN 0 19 564077 2

Typeset by Rastrixi, New Delhi 110 070
Printed in India at Pauls Press., New Delhi 110 020
and published by Manzar Khan, Oxford University Press
YMCA Library Building, Jai Singh Road, New Delhi 110 001

Copyright Statement

Scintilla Publishers for:
Smita Agarwal's poem
'The Planetoid', published in *The Scoria*, vol. 1, no. 2, January 1996

Oxford University Press for:
Imtiaz Dharker's poems
'Purdah I', 'Battle Line', published in *Purdah and Other Poems*, 1989

Kamala Das for:
'The Doubt', 'The Maggots', 'Three P.M.', 'The Joss-sticks at Cadell Road' and 'The Looking Glass', published in *The Descendants* (Writers Workshop, 1967)

Mamta Kalia for:
'Tribute to Papa', 'Sheer Good Luck', 'Compulsions', 'Made for Each Other', 'Sunday Song', 'Brat', 'Dubious Lovers' and 'Positive Thinking', published in *Tribute to Papa and Other Poems* (Writers Workshop, 1970)
'After Eight Years of Marriage', published in *Poems '78* (Writers Workshop, 1978)
'Anonymous', published in *Hers: An Anthology of Poetry in English by Indian Women*, ed. Mary Ann Dasgupta (Writers Workshop, 1978)

Melanie Silgardo for:
'1956–1876 A Poem', 'Stationary Stop', 'Child', 'For Father on the Shelf' and 'The Earthworm's Story', published in *Three Poets* (Newground, 1978)
'Do Not Tell the Children', 'Skies of Design', 'Doris', 'Cat' and 'Bird Broken', published in *Skies of Design* (The College Press, London, 1985)

Eunice de Souza for:
'Catholic Mother', 'Miss Louise', 'For a Child, Not Clever' and 'Autobiographical', published in *Fix* (Newground, 1979)
'Pilgrim' and 'The Road', published in *Women in Dutch Painting* (Praxis, 1988)
'Bequest', published in *Ways of Belonging* (Polygon, Edinburgh, 1990)
'Landscape', 'Outside Jaisalmer' and 'It's Time to Find a Place', published in *Selected and New Poems*, ed. Keith Fernandes (A Department of English, St Xavier's College publication, 1994)

Smita Agarwal for:
'The Lie of the Land: A Letter to Chatwin', 'The Salesman', 'Daywatch in the Scriptorium', 'Mediatrix' and 'Discord', from her unpublished ms 'Glitch'

Tara Patel for:
'Woman', 'Request', 'Calangute Beach, Goa II', 'In Bombay' and 'In a Working Women's Hostel', published in *Single Woman* (Rupa and Co., 1991)

vi

Contents

INTRODUCTION	1
KAMALA DAS	7
From *Summer in Calcutta*	
An Introduction	10
From *The Descendants*	
The Descendants	11
Luminol	12
The Doubt	12
The Maggots	13
Three P.M.	13
The Joss-sticks at Cadell Road	14
The Looking Glass	15
From *The Old Playhouse and Other Poems*	
The Old Playhouse	15
The Stone Age	16
MAMTA KALIA	18
From *Tribute to Papa and Other Poems*	
Tribute to Papa	20
Sheer Good Luck	21
Compulsions	21
Made for Each Other	22
Sunday Song	22
Brat	24
Dubious Lovers	24
Positive Thinking	25
From *Poems '78*	
After Eight Years of Marriage	25
From *Hers*	
Anonymous	26
MELANIE SILGARDO	27
From *Three Poets*	
1956–1976 A Poem	29
Stationary Stop	29
Child	30

For Father on the Shelf 31
The Earthworm's Story 33
From *Skies of Design*
Do Not Tell the Children 33
Skies of Design 34
Doris 34
Cat 35
Bird Broken 36

EUNICE DE SOUZA 37
From *Fix*
Catholic Mother 39
Miss Louise 39
For a Child, Not Clever 40
Autobiographical 41
From *Women in Dutch Painting*
Pilgrim 42
The Road 43
From *Ways of Belonging*
Bequest 43
From *Selected and New Poems*
Landscape 44
Outside Jaisalmer 46
It's Time to Find a Place 47

IMTIAZ DHARKER 48
From *Purdah*
Purdah I 50
Battle-line 51
From *Postcards from god*
Words Find Mouths 53
Living Space 54
Eggplant 55
Namesake 55
8 January 1993 56
The List 57
Minority 58

SMITA AGARWAL 60
From 'Glitch'
The Lie of the Land: A Letter to Chatwin 62
The Salesman 63

The Planetoid   63
Daywatch in the Scriptorium   64
The Word-worker   65
A Grass Widow's Prayer   65
Mediatrix   66
'Our foster-nurse of nature is repose'   67
Discord   67

SUJATA BHATT   69
  From *Brunizem*
    The Peacock   73
    For Paula Modersohn-Becker 1876–1907   74
    The Women of Leh are such —   75
    A Different History   75
    Something for Plato   76
    Iris   77
  From *Monkey Shadows*
    White Asparagus   78
    Kankaria Lake   79

CHARMAYNE D'SOUZA   82
  From *A Spelling Guide to Woman*
    When God First Made a Whore   84
    The White Line Down the Road to Minnesota   85
    I Would Like to Have a Movie Cowboy
    for a Husband   86
    Strange Bedfellows   86
    God's Will?   87
    Judith   88

TARA PATEL   89
  From *Single Woman*
    Woman   90
    Request   90
    Calangute Beach, Goa II   91
    In Bombay   92
    In a Working Women's Hostel   93

Index of First Lines   95

Introduction

Our poetic ancestors are not necessarily those who come just before us in time. Sarojini Naidu's confidently mindless versifying has little to teach contemporary poets, and Toru Dutt did not live long enough to outgrow sentimental pastiche, though she, like Sarojini Naidu, was trying to combine the use of English with 'Indian' themes.

Women have been writing poetry in India since about 1000 BC on religious and secular themes, and it is among these rather more distant ancestors that contemporary women writers are likely to find congenial voices and styles. Among the hymns in the Vedas attributed to women is one by Apala who was rejected by her husband because she had a disfiguring skin disease. She prays to Indra in fairly explicit terms: 'Make these three places sprout, O Indra; my daddy's head and field, and this part of me below my waist.'[1] *Psalms of the Sisters*,[2] and Margaret Macnicol's more general selection *Poems by Indian Women*[3] introduce us to poems by Buddhist nuns who were once married, or homeless, or courtesans, and who rejoice in the freedom they have found in their new life. One of them is relieved that she has left behind 'kitchen drudgery' and a 'brutal husband'.[4] Another is annoyed that monks consider nuns inferior, expressing their contempt by referring to 'woman's two-finger wit'.[5] A commentator points out that the number of poems by nuns which are concerned with liberty is much higher than those by monks.[6]

Again, many examples of unconventionality are provided by *bhakti* women poets in different parts of the country. They are almost too numerous to name but some are of particular interest. Jana Bai, for instance, establishes a very comradely relationship

[1] *The Rig Veda*, translated and annotated by Wendy O'Flaherty, Penguin Books, Harmondsworth, 1981, pp. 256–7.

[2] Translated by Mrs C.A.F. Rhys–Davids, Pali Text Society, London, 1909.

[3] *Poems by Indian Women*, Association Press, Calcutta, 1923.

[4] Ibid., p. 44.

[5] C.A.F. Rhys–Davids (ed.), *Poems of Cloister and Jungle*, John Murray, London, 1941, p. 30.

[6] Ibid., pp. 30–1.

1

with Krishna whom she sometimes calls Vithoba or Vitabai. She makes him help with the housework, rub down her aching back, and clean her hair when it is full of lice. Some of the confidence felt by women of outcaste status can be heard in the work of a woman called Chokha's Wife. 'Without defilement', she says, 'Is no flesh created.'[7]

In Sanskrit, a woman called Silabhattarika, of whom nothing is known, regrets the fact that she married the man who was her lover, because their love-making has become so much less interesting than it was before.[8] Another poem, also by a woman (Bhava-devi), writing in Sanskrit on a similar theme, reads:

> At first our bodies knew a perfect oneness,
> but then grew two:
> the lover, you,
> and I, unhappy I, the loved.
> Now you are the husband, I the wife.
> What else should come of this my life,
> a tree too hard to break,
> if not such bitter fruit.[9]

Prakrit poems written by women or in the voices of women are often sexually explicit in a way that few modern women can match:

> Woman wanting
> more
> not having come
> seeing a cart in the middle
> of the village
> oh blessed indeed
> says the hub of the wheel
> with the axle in it
> all the time[10]

Research into oral traditions has revealed women's versions of the *Ramayana* which foreground and develop aspects of the

[7] *Poems by Indian Women*, p. 49.

[8] *The Peacock's Egg*, translated by W.S. Merwin and Moussaieff Masson, North Point Press, San Francisco, 1981, p. 112.

[9] Daniel Ingalls (ed.), *Sanskrit Poetry*, Harvard University Press, Cambridge Massachusetts, 1972, p. 25.

[10] David Smith, 'Classical Sanskrit Poetry and the Modern Reader', *Contributions to South Asian Studies* 2, Oxford University Press, Delhi, 1982, p. 10.

narrative which would be of interest to women. As Velcheru Narayana Rao who has researched this material in Telugu observes, what one gets from these poems and songs is a picture of a 'complex joint family where life is filled with tension and fear, frustration and suspicion, as well as with love, affection, and tenderness'.[11] The language is 'deceptively gentle . . . the underlying meanings reveal an atmosphere of subdued tensions, hidden sexuality, and frustrated emotions'.[12]

Curiously, when we come to Sarojini Naidu we find some ambiguities in her attitudes. Though she campaigned against purdah, her poem 'Purdah' is imbued with nostalgia and exotic appeal: 'Her life is a revolving dream / Of languid and sequestered ease . . . '[13] And even James Cousins, a friend of the poet's, was moved to protest against some of her work 'because of its perpetuation of the "door-mat" attitude to womanhood . . . that masculine domination has sentimentalised into a virtue'.[14] He quotes from a love poem which ends with the lines:

> Sweeter shall my wild heart rest
> With your footprints on my breast.

The nine poets included in this anthology represent two generations of post-1947 poets. What they have achieved can be appreciated partly by contrast, not just with the Dutts and Sarojini Naidu, but with the numerous poets who tend to be included in anthologies for documentary purposes, or with the intention of being comprehensive. P. Lal's *Modern Indian Poetry in English: An Anthology and a Credo* included 132 poets, 31 of whom were women, and most of whom have dropped out of sight. The simpering tone of some of the entries on women poets is still something of a shock: 'Miss Bubli Sen. Love(s) painting, and has made a hobby of psychology.'[15] There is a large photograph of Ms Sen, two pages

---

[11] 'A Ramayana of Their Own', in Paula Richman (ed.), *Many Ramayanas*, Oxford University Press, Delhi, 1994, p. 129.

[12] Ibid., p. 129.

[13] G. Galway Turnbull (ed.), *Selected Poems*, Oxford University Press, Bombay, 1930, p. 72.

[14] James Cousins, 'The Poetry of Sarojini Naidu', *The Renaissance in India*, Ganesh and Co., Madras, 1918, pp. 261–2.

[15] P. Lal (ed.), *Modern Indian Poetry in English: An Anthology and a Credo*, Writers Workshop, Calcutta, 1969, p. 509.

of her thoughts about writing in English, and one very short poem which reads like this:

> Where was I going to?
> Oh yes, through the field,
> over the fence — to the other side.[16]

V.K. Gokak's *The Golden Treasury of Indo-Anglian Poetry 1828–1965*,[17] had at least the excuse of being a documentary anthology. It begins with Henry Derozio, and goes on to include ten women poets. The work of many of these confirms the fact that the poets nearest the moderns in time are the least congenial in tone and idiom. Lotika Ghose, for example, writes:

> I have wandered forlorn in life's waste desolate places, . . .
> Which lyred me on through an all-supporting Void,
> The soul of a Godhead omnipotent, lone,
> Guarding the riddle of created things . . . [18]

Hers, an anthology of women poets writing in English, edited by Mary Ann Dasgupta was published by Writers Workshop in 1978. Of the 32 poets included, only Kamala Das's work, and a poem by Mamta Kalia ('Anonymous', included here) still survive scrutiny in terms of language and craftsmanship.

More recently, Arlene Zidé's *In Their Own Voice* includes 140 women poets writing in various languages in India. About half-a-dozen or so of these write in English, and the anthology has the merit of putting the work by women writing poetry in English in the wider context of concern 'with the more "modern" issues of relationship/personality/self-exploration/political and social consciousness'.[19] Zidé's anthology, incidentally, is one of only two anthologies published in India which includes the work of Melanie Silgardo, a pioneer in writing and publishing poetry. The only other anthology to do so is *Bequest*,[20] an anthology of contemporary poets from St Xavier's College, Bombay.

[16] Ibid., p. 510.
[17] V.K. Gokak (ed.), *The Golden Treasury of Indo-Anglian Poetry 1828–1965*, Sahitya Akademi, New Delhi, 1970.
[18] Ibid., p. 173.
[19] Arlene Zidé and Aruna Sitesh (eds), *In Their Own Voice*, Penguin India, Delhi, 1993, p. xxxi.
[20] Keith Fernandes and Eunice de Souza (eds), *Bequest*, A Department of English St Xavier's Publication, Bombay, 1992.

Arvind Krishna Mehrotra who once remarked in a review that 'the rate of mortality among the Indian poets in English must be the highest anywhere',[21] reduces the number of women poets represented in his anthology *Twelve Modern Indian Poets* to one.[22] What is important about this anthology, however, is its crisp introduction, the clear focus on language and craftsmanship, rather than on thematic content. This focus is a welcome relief after, for instance, Vilas Sarang's dated and woolly ideas about 'Indianness' and the "dangers" inherent in women's writing about the self, in his anthology *Indian English Poetry Since 1950* (Orient Longman, 1990).

Women Writing in India does not include any women poets writing in English on the grounds that their work 'is more easily available to the reader'.[23] This is not true, in fact. Even libraries which are required by law to stock all books published in India have virtually nothing because publishers do not concern themselves with this law. Publishing co-operatives created by poets have produced beautiful books, reasonably priced, but their distribution system is usually very poor.

Friends living abroad eventually helped me out by mailing Indian books to India. If a poet such as Melanie Silgardo came to be widely known in spite of the unavailability of her work, it is largely because of Bruce King's discussions in his *Modern Indian Poetry in English*, (OUP, Delhi, 1987), and to a smaller extent because of poetry readings in Bombay which included her work even after she left to live in London. Again, it is amazing that a fine poet such as Smita Agarwal who has been writing for twenty years has not yet published her first manuscript 'Glitch'.

This anthology includes poets who I feel have extended both the subject matter and the idiom of poetry. Some of them live abroad, some live and work here. The notes on each poet attempt to provide a context, raise questions, and provide possible areas of discussion suggested by the work: ancestors, the effect of ideologies, the pressures of multiculturalism, attitudes to the craft of writing. The order in which the poets appear follows

21 *The Times of India*, 10 February 1980, p. 12.

22 *The Oxford India Anthology of Twelve Modern Indian Poets*, Oxford University Press, Delhi, 1992.

23 Susie Tharu and K. Lalitha (eds), *Women Writing in India 600 BC to the Present*, Oxford University Press, Delhi, 1991, p. xxiv.

the publication dates of first books, except in the case of Smita Agarwal who has not yet published a book.

I have mentioned that this anthology consists of two generations of women poets in India. In fact, phrases used to describe 'the new generation of poets', publishing in the eighties and nineties, can describe the older generation equally well: 'unafraid, motivated, clear-sighted, and they use English with a sense of ease. Their language, style, rhythms and forms are inventive, original, and contemporary.'[24] There is, in addition, a wide range of subjects — time, history, social problems, religious search, the environment, painters, writers, language.

The brief for this anthology is a limited number of Indian women poets writing in English, the number being limited to allow for adequate representation of the variety in each poet's work. This obviously makes the anthology different in scope from those which seek to represent the many women writing by including at least one poem by each. There are many recent poets who have written a few good poems but not published a book. They could not be included partly for reasons of space, partly for the reason that I prefer to wait a while to see how much staying power they have. Some prize-winning poets have not been included because the poem that won the prize turned out to be the only viable one. Some much-published poets have been excluded because their work is turgid or flat. Anthologists invariably make enemies. Nevertheless it is hoped that this collection, with its range of poignant, witty, ironic, technically assured poems will give the reader as much pleasure as it gives the anthologist.

[24] Sudeep Sen, 'Modern Indian Poetry: The New Generation', *Poetry Review*, vol. 83, no. 1, Spring 1993.

Kamala Das

Born 1934. Kamala Das's published collections include *Summer in Calcutta* in 1965, *The Descendants* in 1967, *The Old Playhouse and Other Poems* in 1973 and *Only the Soul Knows How to Sing* in 1996. With Pritish Nandy she published *Tonight This Savage Rite: The Love Poetry of Kamala Das and Pritish Nandy*, 1979; *Collected Poems* was published in 1984, and her autobiography *My Story* in 1976. She has published several novels and short stories in Malayalam, under the pen name Madhavikutty. Some of these are available in translation. Her *Alphabet of Lust* (1977) is a novel in English. Also in English are two collections of short stories, *A Doll for the Child Prostitute*, 1977, and *Padmavati the Harlot and Other Stories*, 1992. She was awarded a P.E.N. Prize in 1964, the Kerala Sahitya Akademi Award for fiction in 1969, the Chaman Lal award for journalism in 1971, the Asian World Prize for Literature in 1985, and the Indira Priyadarshini Vrikshamitra Award in 1988. She was awarded an Honorary Doctorate by the World Academy of Arts and Culture, Taiwan, in 1984.

Kamala Das's publication of her autobiography *My Story*[1] has encouraged readers to check the poems against the life. But it is not useful, finally, to read back from the poetry into the life, in the case of Kamala Das or any other 'confessional' poet. The 'I' of the autobiography is as much a persona as the 'I' of the poems. While Kamala Das plays out her various roles in the poems, unhappy woman, unhappy wife, reluctant nymphomaniac, she also talks of the 'sad lie / of my unending lust',[2] a line which cautions us against thinking we have got at the 'truth' of this apparently forthright persona.

Critical concern tends to be equally divided between Kamala Das's morals and her grammar, her public critique of her husband and her cavalier attitude to the definite article. Vrinda Nabar, in a recent book on Kamala Das, *The Endless Female Hungers*,[3] writes

[1] Sterling, New Delhi, 1976.
[2] 'In Love', *Summer in Calcutta*, Rajinder Paul, New Delhi, 1965, p. 14.
[3] Sterling, New Delhi, 1994.

with pursed lips, frequent exclamation marks and an exasperated desire to tidy up what she sees as Das's lazy sentences, tiresome attitudes, and penchant for role playing. Apparently, Kamala Das 'speaks at length about her pet poodle',[4] and 'remarks that even her perspiration smelt musky'.[5] Das's lines — 'I asked my husband / am I hetero / am I lesbian / or am I just plain frigid? / He only laughed . . . ' — earns from Nabar the schoolmarmish comment: 'One can hardly blame him!'[6]

It is the considered opinion of another critic that Kamala Das is 'less an artist than a human being'.[7] Opinions like this stem directly from T.S. Eliot's theory of 'impersonality' which has tremendous prestige here, though it was written in another place and time. More interestingly, Kamala Das's forthrightness is attributed to her Nayar background.[8]

The poet Carol Rumens finds it interesting that this bilingual writer 'uses both Malayalam and English for her fiction, but English only for her poetry, a factor which suggests that English is her mother-tongue. The voice operates between ideolect and dialect. It is outside standard norms of poetic diction, yet inward enough with the language to conjure a sense of these more familiar dialects, sometimes assimilated, sometimes hovering at the edge'.[9] But Rumens does at the same time wonder about possible 'vernacular oddities'.[10]

Women writers owe a special debt to Kamala Das. She mapped out the terrain for post-colonial women in social and linguistic terms. Whatever her vernacular oddities, she has spared us the colonial cringe. She has also spared us what in some circles, nativist and expatriate, is still considered mandatory: the politically correct 'anguish' of writing in English. And in her best poems she speaks for women, certainly, but also for anyone who has known pain, inadequacy, despair. She is capable of handling varied effects: the brooding intensity of 'The Old Playhouse'

4 Ibid., Preface, p. vi.

5 Ibid., p. 11.

6 Ibid., pp. 51–2.

7 Anisur Rahman, *Expressive Form in the Poetry of Kamala Das*, Abhinav Publications, New Delhi, 1981, p. 76.

8 R. Parthasarathy, 'Indian Verse: The Making of a Tradition', in *Alien Voice*, Avadesh K. Srivastava (ed.), Print House, Lucknow, 1991, p. 50.

9 'Dislocated Carnality', *Poetry Review*, vol. 83, no. 1, Spring 1993, p. 35.

10 Ibid.

which brings together all her major concerns, the search for love, the power politics of relationships, the controlled tenderness of 'Three P.M.' and the acerbity of 'The Proud One'[11] in which the speaker observes her man 'Lying nailed to his bed in imitation/of the great crucifixion'.

Meanwhile Kamala Das, who has become an activist in the cause of social issues, tells Peter Forbes, in an interview:[12] 'I'm a politician not a poet.' Sarojini Naidu too moved from poetry to politics, but the resemblance ends there.

---

[11] *The Descendants*, Writers Workshop, Calcutta, 1967, p. 18.
[12] 'In Search of Kavita', *Poetry Review*, vol. 83, no. 1, Spring 1993, p. 5.

from *Summer in Calcutta*

An Introduction

I don't know politics but I know the names
Of those in power, and can repeat them like
Days of week, or names of months, beginning with
Nehru. I am Indian, very brown, born in
Malabar, I speak three languages, write in
Two, dream in one. Don't write in English, they said,
English is not your mother-tongue. Why not leave
Me alone, critics, friends, visiting cousins,
Every one of you? Why not let me speak in
Any language I like? The language I speak
Becomes mine, its distortions, its queernesses
All mine, mine alone. It is half English, half
Indian, funny perhaps, but it is honest,
It is as human as I am human, don't
You see? It voices my joys, my longings, my
Hopes, and it is useful to me as cawing
Is to crows or roaring to the lions, it
Is human speech, the speech of the mind that is
Here and not there, a mind that sees and hears and
Is aware. Not the deaf, blind speech
Of trees in storm or of monsoon clouds or of rain or the
Incoherent mutterings of the blazing
Funeral pyre. I was child, and later they
Told me I grew, for I became tall, my limbs
Swelled and one or two places sprouted hair. When
I asked for love, not knowing what else to ask
For, he drew a youth of sixteen into the
Bedroom and closed the door. He did not beat me
But my sad woman-body felt so beaten.

The weight of my breasts and womb crushed me. I shrank
Pitifully. Then . . . I wore a shirt and my
Brother's trousers, cut my hair short and ignored
My womanliness. Dress in sarees, be girl
Be wife, they said. Be embroiderer, be cook,

10

Be a quarreller with servants. Fit in. Oh,
Belong, cried the categorizers. Don't sit
On walls or peep in through our lace-draped windows.
Be Amy, or be Kamala. Or, better
Still, be Madhavikutty. It is time to
Choose a name, a role. Don't play pretending games.
Don't play at schizophrenia or be a
Nympho. Don't cry embarrassingly loud when
Jilted in love . . . I met a man, loved him. Call
Him not by any name, he is every man
Who wants a woman, just as I am every
Woman who seeks love. In him . . . the hungry haste
Of rivers, in me . . . the oceans' tireless
Waiting. Who are you, I ask each and everyone,
The answer is, it is I. Anywhere and,
Everywhere, I see the one who calls himself
If in this world, he is tightly packed like the
Sword in its sheath. It is I who drink lonely
Drinks at twelve, midnight, in hotels of strange towns,
It is I who laugh, it is I who make love
And then, feel shame, it is I who lie dying
With a rattle in my throat. I am sinner,
I am saint. I am the beloved and the
Betrayed. I have no joys which are not yours, no
Aches which are not yours. I too call myself I.

from *The Descendants*

The Descendants

We have spent our youth in gentle sinning
Exchanging some insubstantial love and
Often thought we were hurt, but no pain in
Us could remain, no bruise could scar or
Even slightly mar our cold loveliness.
We have lain in every weather, nailed, no, not
To crosses, but to soft beds and against
Softer forms, while the heaving, lurching,

Tender hours passed in a half-dusk, half-dawn and
Half-dream, half-real trance. We were the yielders,
Yielding ourselves to everything. It is
Not for us to scrape the walls of wombs for
Memories, not for us even to
Question death, but as child to mother's arms
We shall give ourselves to the fire or to
The hungry earth to be slowly eaten,
Devoured. None will step off his cross
Or show his wounds to us, no god lost in
Silence shall begin to speak, no lost love
Claim us, no, we are not going to be
Ever redeemed, or made new.

Luminol

Love-lorn,
It is only
Wise at times, to let sleep
Make holes in memory, even
If it
Be the cold and
Luminous sleep banked in
The heart of pills, for he shall not
Enter,
Your ruthless one,
Being human, clumsy
With noise and movement, the soul's mute
Arena,
That silent sleep inside your sleep.

The Doubt

When a man is dead, or a woman,
We call the corpse not he
Or she but it. Does it
Not mean that we believe
That only the souls have sex and that

Sex is invisible?
Then the question is, who
Is the man, who the girl,
All sex-accessories being no
Indication. Is she
A male who with frail hands
Clasps me to her breast, while
The silence in her sickroom, turning
Eloquent, accuses
Me of ingratitude?
And, is he female who
After love, smoothes out the bed sheets with
Finicky hands and plucks
From pillows strands of hair?
. . . How well I can see him
After a murder, conscientiously
Tidy up the scene, wash
The bloodstains under
Faucet, bury the knife . . .
And, what am I in sex who shuttles
Obsessively from his
Stabs to recovery
In her small silent room?

The Maggots

At sunset, on the river bank, Krishna
Loved her for the last time and left . . .

That night in her husband's arms, Radha felt
So dead that he asked, What is wrong,
Do you mind my kisses, love? and she said,
No, not at all, but thought, What is
It to the corpse if the maggots nip?

Three P.M.

It was only in sleep that he
Showed his little-boy loneliness.

And, coming upon it one afternoon
I could not bear to wake him, even though

Our private hours were rationed
Then. But sat, watching, wondering
In what tortuous lanes of dream he walked, this
Innocent, so bewildered by his lust.

The Joss-sticks at Cadell Road

Near the sea behind Cadell Road
They burn as joss-sticks
The poor men's bodies
Those dark, thin corpses
All bound with strings of tuberose
And the brilliant marigold.
We saw them bring one, last Sunday
An hour after our
Tea-time, scented up
To smell like a low-paid
Street girl, while some crones followed
Wailing flatly and
Monotonously
As only the poor
And the absolutely
Hopeless know how to wail. When
They fed the body
To the fire, the fire
Leapt high, snarling beast-like. Then
The corpse-bearers threw
The garlands into
The sea. A queue of
Sea-gulls rode the waves.
My husband said, I think I shall
Have a beer, it's hot,
Very hot today.
And I thought, I must
Drive fast to town and
Lie near my friend for an hour. I
Badly need some rest.

14

The Looking Glass

Getting a man to love you is easy
Only be honest about your wants as
Woman. Stand nude before the glass with him
So that he sees himself the stronger one
And believes it so, and you so much more
Softer, younger, lovelier . . . Admit your
Admiration. Notice the perfection
Of his limbs, his eyes reddening under
Shower, the shy walk across the bathroom floor,
Dropping towels, and the jerky way he
Urinates. All the fond details that make
Him male and your only man. Gift him all,
Gift him what makes you woman, the scent of
Long hair, the musk of sweat between the breasts,
The warm shock of menstrual blood, and all your
Endless female hungers. Oh yes, getting
A man to love is easy, but living
Without him afterward may have to be
Faced. A living without life when you move
Around, meeting strangers, with your eyes that
Gave up their search, with ears that hear only
His last voice calling out your name and your
Body which once under his touch had gleamed
Like burnished brass, now drab and destitute.

from *The Old Playhouse and Other Poems*

The Old Playhouse

You planned to tame a swallow, to hold her
In the long summer of your love so that she would forget
Not the raw seasons alone, and the homes left behind, but
Also her nature, the urge to fly, and the endless
Pathways of the sky. It was not to gather knowledge
Of yet another man that I came to you but to learn
What I was, and by learning, to learn to grow, but every

15

Lesson you gave was about yourself. You were pleased
With my body's response, its weather, its usual shallow
Convulsions. You dribbled spittle into my mouth, you poured
Yourself into every nook and cranny, you embalmed
My poor lust with your bitter-sweet juices. You called me wife,
I was taught to break saccharine into your tea and
To offer at the right moment the vitamins. Cowering
Beneath your monstrous ego I ate the magic loaf and
Became a dwarf. I lost my will and reason, to all your
Questions I mumbled incoherent replies. The summer
Begins to pall. I remember the ruder breezes
Of the fall and the smoke from burning leaves. Your room is
Always lit by artificial lights, your windows always
Shut. Even the air-conditioner helps so little,
All pervasive is the male scent of your breath. The cut flowers
In the vases have begun to smell of human sweat. There is
No more singing, no more a dance, my mind is an old
Playhouse with all its lights put out. The strong man's
technique is
Always the same, he serves his love in lethal doses,
For, love is Narcissus at the water's edge, haunted
By its own lonely face, and yet it must seek at last
An end, a pure, total freedom, it must will the mirrors
To shatter and the kind night to erase the water.

The Stone Age

Fond husband, ancient settler in the mind,
Old fat spider, weaving webs of bewilderment,
Be kind. You turn me into a bird of stone, a granite
Dove, you build round me a shabby drawing room,
And stroke my pitted face absent-mindedly while
You read. With loud talk you bruise my pre-morning sleep,
You stick a finger into my dreaming eye. And
Yet, on daydreams, strong men cast their shadows, they sink
Like white suns in the swell of my Dravidian blood,
Secretly flow the drains beneath sacred cities.
When you leave, I drive my blue battered car

16

Along the bluer sea. I run up the forty
Noisy steps to knock at another's door.
Through peep-holes, the neighbours watch,
they watch me come
And go like rain. Ask me, everybody, ask me
What he sees in me, ask me why he is called a lion,
A libertine, ask me the flavour of his
Mouth, ask me why his hand sways like a hooded snake
Before it clasps my pubis. Ask me why like
A great tree, felled, he slumps against my breasts,
And sleeps. Ask me why life is short and love is
Shorter still, ask me what is bliss and what its price. . . .

(*Opinion*)

Mamta Kalia

Born 1940. An M.A. in English Literature, Delhi University, 1963, Mamta Kalia writes poetry in English and in Hindi. Her books in English are *Tribute to Papa* (1970), and *Poems '78* (1978). In Hindi she has five novels to her credit, seven short story collections, two one-act play collections, four novelettes for children, and three works which she has edited. She has won six awards for her writing in Hindi. She was an Advisory Member on the Sahitya Akademi Board, New Delhi from 1988–91, and is a member of several other boards. She is a regular broadcaster for Akashvani and Doordarshan. She is at present Principal of Mahila Seva Sadan Degree College in Allahabad.

While Kamala Das feels an emotional–sexual compulsion to 'take in with greed, like a forest-fire that / Consumes', Mamta Kalia feels a compulsion to 'pick my nose / in a public place'. Part of the pleasure of reading Mamta Kalia's first book in English *Tribute to Papa* comes from its relaxed attitude to poetry, its wit, its understated irony, its played-down persona to whom nothing has happened 'except two children / and two miscarriages'. Nor are the parents mythologized. Papa is an 'unsuccessful man' who 'couldn't wangle a cosy place in the world', and mama can scarcely be 'proud of your creativity — / Except for the comfort / That I looked like Papa / And not like the neighbour / Who shared our bathroom'.

Bruce King has remarked, rightly, that 'the present contemporary manner appears to have been initiated by Mamta Kalia . . .'[1] He goes on to add that 'the directness of expression and natural, idiomatic colloquial vigour is more often found in the verse of Das, Kalia, de Souza and Silgardo than in the male Indian English poets'.[2] He should have added something about a line of wit in Indian poetry in English by women. There is a fair amount of it both in the work included and work that it was not possible to

[1] *Modern Indian Poetry in English*, Oxford University Press, Delhi, 1987, p. 155.
[2] Ibid., p. 161.

include. Wit is sometimes an underestimated quality in poetry. One gets the occasional student who says, 'Yes, funny. But where's the poetry?', unaware that wit demands as much of a sense of timing as any other kind of writing.

Mamta Kalia is the only poet in this collection who writes poems both in English and in Hindi. In a letter she says she has 'no transit problems'. She says she was more involved in writing in English when she lived in Bombay, but in Allahabad, the 'nerve centre of Hindi writing', her emphasis shifted to Hindi. In Allahabad she was 'primarily affected by the very ordinary life-style of extraordinary intellectuals, and their critical concepts and concerns'. Allahabad is one place in the land, she adds, 'that leaves you alone to create or vegetate. I chose creation'.

One cannot comment on Mamta Kalia's poems in Hindi on the basis of two poems which she translated on request, and sent by return post. One is about her father, the other about women, both subjects she has dealt with in English. However, if one were to offer an opinion, one could say that the poems in English work better. They are tightly constructed and make their points more economically. Her English poems as her Hindi ones reveal that few writers can capture the tragicomic nitty-gritty of routine the way Mamta Kalia can. One line from 'Women', originally written in Hindi, demonstrates this: 'They expertly alter Munna's trousers into Pappu's knickers.' These women belong to the large tribe of Kalia women who 'see worthless movies at reduced rates/and feel happy at reduced rates'. As always, the wit both controls and enhances the sadness.

from *Tribute to Papa and Other Poems*

Tribute to Papa

Who cares for you, Papa?
Who cares for your clean thoughts, clean
                    words, clean teeth?
Who wants to be an angel like you?
Who wants it?

You are an unsuccessful man, Papa.
Couldn't wangle a cosy place in the world.
You've always lived a life of limited dreams.

I wish you had guts, Papa;
To smuggle eighty thousand watches at a stroke,
And I'd proudly say, 'My father's in import-
                    export business, you know.'
I'd be proud of you then.

But you've always wanted to be a model man,
A sort of an ideal.
When you can't think of doing anything,
You start praying,
Spending useless hours at the temple.

You want me to be like you, Papa,
Or like Rani Lakshmibai.
You're not sure what greatness is,
But you want me to be great.

I give two donkey-claps for your greatness.
And three for Rani Lakshmibai.

These days I am seriously thinking of
                    disowning you, Papa,
You and your sacredness.
What if I start calling you Mr Kapur, Lower
            Division Clerk, Accounts Section?

Everything about you clashes with nearly
                    everything about me.
You suspect I am having a love-affair these days,

20

But you're too shy to have it confirmed.
What if my tummy starts showing gradually
And I refuse to have it curetted?
But I'll be careful, Papa,
Or I know you'll at once think of suicide.

Sheer Good Luck

So many things
could have happened to me.
I could have been kidnapped
at the age of seven
and ravaged by
dirty-minded middle-aged men.
I could have been married off
to a man with a bad smell
and turned frigid
as a frigidaire.
I could have been
an illiterate woman
putting thumb-prints
on rent-receipts.
But nothing ever happened to me
except two children
and two miscarriages.

Compulsions

I want to pick my nose
in a public place
I want to sit in my office chair
with my feet up
I want to slap the boy
who makes love in a cafe
while I wait alone for the waiter
to bring me coffee and sandwiches
I want to pay Sunday visits
totally undressed

I want to throw away
all my cosmetics
I want to reveal
my real age

Made for Each Other

How close we felt
discussing our dislikes,
sharing a few hatreds,
comparing notes about enemies.
I was elated to find
you couldn't stand *The Faerie Queene*,
dahi vadās and arranged marriages.
And you were delighted to see me
in an ill-fitting kurta,
a fag and minus-four glasses.
You said you hated pretty girls:
they were dull, silly and egoistic.
I said, 'Boys, they are horrors,
they grow sideburns and weigh so little.'
You said, 'Let's get married
and damn the world.'

Sunday Song

The calendar has just dropped
a Sunday in my room.
I'm puzzled how to hold on
to this long vacant day.
There's a lot of dirty linen
and many pending phone calls.
On the table, there's a shaky
                    mountain
                    of
                    books,

and I have to wash my hair too.
I know I won't attend to any of these.
Every now and then
I'll ask my room-mate the time,
and pretend to be sleepy.
I know that in other rooms
the girls are dressing up devotedly.
Looking at them you can easily tell
with whom they plan to go out.
But ask them and they will say,
'A cousin has come from Bhavanagar.'

I wonder at the emptiness
of this Sunday and of all Sundays.
It was never like this
when you were here.
We'd rise late,
sip each other's tea,
bathe together,
quarrel,
all in a few hours.
We'd go places, visit friends, eat *bhel puri,*
We'd come back, make love again, call it a day.

I don't know how it has happened
but the road seems narrower without you,
and the sea less dignified.
I can't talk to a soul
without mentioning you.
You know how it bores them.
No one wants a moping matron around.
In reality
all our friends were your friends,
all our ideas your ideas
all our projects your projects.
I followed you like a corollary.
Now I am away from you,
missing my handcuffs,
feeling stupid
on this long unpromising Sunday.

Brat

Looking at my navel
I'm reminded of you, Mamma.
How I lay suspended
By that cordial cord inside you.
I must have been a rattish thing,
A wriggly roll of shallow breath.
You, perhaps, were hardly proud
Of your creativity —
Except for the comfort
That I looked like Papa
And not like the neighbour
Who shared our bathroom.

Dubious Lovers

I'd live you as a Saturday night memory
or a voice over the telephone;
I'd feel close to you then.
But you insist on your presence,
and I am conscious of it
as I am of a burning in my rectum
or of a hair on my chin.
After the first few moments
it gets so gawky,
we look at each other sheepishly
badly needing something to talk about.
Now when I want you to write verses on me
you only compose limericks,
and when you suggest we dine out,
I quickly get busy with its finances.
Every time I open my mouth,
you feel let down,
and every time you discuss your pay scale,
I try hard not to frown.
If this goes on where will we end?
Or have we ended before we have begun?

24

Positive Thinking

Let us forget your death and mine.
We have so much to remember:
A comfortable home
Your air-conditioned office
Our quarter-dozen children
Your bank balance
The Race Course nearby
Your Yoga exercises
My fortnightly manicure
And all those social engagements.
Who cares for primal disappointments?

from *Poems '78*

After Eight Years of Marriage

After eight years of marriage
The first time I visited my parents,
They asked, 'Are you happy, tell us.'
It was an absurd question
And I should have laughed at it.
Instead, I cried,
And in between sobs, nodded yes.
I wanted to tell them
That I was happy on Tuesday.
I was unhappy on Wednesday.
I was happy one day at 8 o'clock
I was most unhappy by 8.15.
I wanted to tell them how one day
We all ate a watermelon and laughed.
I wanted to tell them how I wept in bed all night once
And struggled hard from hurting myself.
That it wasn't easy to be happy in a family of twelve.
But they were looking at my two sons,
Hopping around like young goats.

Their wrinkled hands, beaten faces and grey eyelashes
Were all too much too real.
So I swallowed everything,
And smiled a smile of great content.

from *Hers*

Anonymous

I no longer feel I'm Mamta Kalia.
I'm Kamla
or Vimla
or Kanta or Shanta.
I cook, I wash,
I bear, I rear,
I nag, I wag,
I sulk, I sag.
I see worthless movies at reduced rates
and feel happy at reduced rates.
I get a free plastic bucket
with a large packet of Super-Surf,
and feel happy.
I put on weight every month
like Kamla or Vimla
or Kanta or Shanta,
and feel happy.
I am no longer Mamta Kalia.

Melanie Silgardo

Born 1956. Melanie Silgardo read English Literature for a B.A. at St Xavier's College, Bombay, and for an M.A. at the University of Bombay. While in Bombay, she worked for Macmillan and various magazines, and founded Newground, a publishing co-operative with Raul D'Gama Rose and Santan Rodrigues. Together they also published their first book, *Three Poets*, in 1978. She then went to do a course at the London College of Printing, after which she became a Commissioning Editor with Virago where she worked from 1988 to 1995. *Skies of Design* (1985) was published in London and was awarded the Best First Book Commonwealth Poetry Prize, Asian Section. She is now taking a break after eighteen years in publishing and is teaching creative writing courses in London. She recently co-tutored an Arvon Foundation Creative Writing course with Marsha Hunt. She edited with Janet Beck *Virago New Poets* in 1993, and *Short Circuits* (1996), an anthology of short fiction. She now works as a freelance editor in London.

Described by Ranjit Hoskote as one of the 'pioneers'[1] of Indian poetry in English, Melanie Silgardo has not been given the recognition she deserves. Her work has been anthologized abroad,[2] but to the best of my knowledge only two anthologies in India have included her: *Bequest*,[3] published by the Department of English, St Xavier's College, Bombay, and *In Their Own Voice*,[4] edited by Arlene Zidé.

Though Melanie Silgardo started writing the poems which appear in *Three Poets* when she was an undergraduate, there is nothing of the apprentice in any of them. The poems are deeply emotional but never mawkish. Stressful states are precisely evoked. 'The Earthworm's Story' reads like a funny–sad spoof on the subject matter and attitudes of confessional poems. And though

[1] 'Voices From Behind the Veil', *The Sunday Times of India*, 7 May 1995.
[2] Wendy Mulford (ed.), *The Virago Book of Love Poetry*, Virago, London, 1990, p. 30.
[3] Edited by Keith Fernandes and Eunice de Souza, Bombay, 1992, pp. 36–8.
[4] Penguin India, Delhi, 1993, p. 225.

27

many poets have written 'grandmother' poems, Silgardo's 'Doris' is distinctive because it is unsentimental, compassionate but not mythified.

Bruce King, commenting on Melanie Silgardo's work in *Modern Indian Poetry in English*, writes, 'An earlier generation of women seemed to feel that the problems of life could be solved through a man's love. In de Souza and Silgardo the women seem to be on their own: If they make a mess of their lives it is their mess and not the fault of a husband or lover. But this must be qualified. Like many contemporary feminist writers, both de Souza and Silgardo are preoccupied with their relationship to their father.'[5]

Perhaps inevitably, because Eunice de Souza was Silgardo's teacher, and because both have a similar Goan Catholic background, comparisons tend to be made between their concerns and approaches. Bruce King finds Silgardo's portrayal of her community 'more compassionate',[6] but comments that both have 'mapped large, previously neglected, areas of Indian reality',[7] and both 'offer a range of highly volatile emotions with poems unexpectedly changing direction and gaining effect from their inner contrasts, conflicts, ironies and extremes',[8] Silgardo's forte being her use of disturbing 'expressionistic'[9] images.

One of Melanie Silgardo's important contributions to the poetry scene in Bombay was the formation, with Santan Rodrigues and Raul D'Gama Rose, of Newground, a publishing co-operative. After publishing *Three Poets*, which consisted of their work, they published Eunice de Souza's *Fix* (1979), Saleem Peeradina's *First Offence* (1980), and Manohar Shetty's *A Guarded Space* (1981).

---

5 *Modern Indian Poetry in English*, Oxford University Press, Delhi, 1987, pp. 159–60.

6 Ibid., p. 133.

7 Ibid., p. 135.

8 Ibid., p. 155.

9 Ibid., p. 134.

from *Three Poets*

1956–1976 A Poem

Twenty years ago
they laid a snare.

I emerged headlong,
embarrassed, wet.
They slapped me
on my bottom,
I screamed.
That was my first experience.

Ambitions gutter now.
Afterthoughts glide by.
My special icicles
rifle through me. For diet
I scratch out eyes.

Under my pillow
a lever
to manipulate dreams.

The insane need
to roll up the sky.
Stand it up
in some convenient place,
hang a picture up instead.
A change from God's blank face.
The end.

Stationary Stop

This station has no name.
No king was born here.
No president died here.

This station breathes with people
who breed each other.

29

There are one way tracks
diverging at the signal 'go'.
No train has ever passed this way.
The commuters have tired
of waiting. They have lost
count of each other.
J. and K. are very much alike,
are they brothers?

Rats burrow through bones.
Scavengers are never hungry.
The perfume of dead flowers
stinks in compromise.
J. and K. *are* brothers, their
mother says so.

When the train arrives
it will be disastrous to say 'go'.
If the people had resources
they would build an airplane.
But the air is crowded too.
In fact J. and K. are identical
twins, they compare in every way.

Today there is hope.
Old men are dressed in
youthful attire. Babies are
still born. A train may come.
It is Sunday.

One man begins to walk.

Child

You hold the toy at me
as if it were the last barrier.
Your little Christmas elephant
with its ears all pink.

You are shy and move away.
So I must stay here for a bit
like the proverbial mountain,

wait till some last smile
can measure your frown and replace it.

Your experience of three years
has made you wise.
And though you know the sun
must daily sink into the sea,
you will not trust my adult face,
my dangling arms.

I talk too fluently,
and smile too often and too long.

But I've not come to stay.
Yet, I can feel the hundred things
you'd like to say
                      choke
as if the alphabets had jagged ends
that fixed inside your throat.

Sometimes, your head on one side
you venture, tentative,
brother of the sparrow.

You won't be kissed.
I too was a child my dear,
my heart as large as your fist.

You smile now,
the mask has taken off your frown.
You have lost your little wisdom.

Child, it won't be long
before you laugh
for the price of a song.

For Father on the Shelf

Father, you will be proud to know
you left something behind.
The year you died
I inherited a mind.

At twelve, the letters you wrote
in a large, scrawling man's hand
became my manifesto.
From time to time
I resurrected you, the days
you went fishing
with your line and bait,
returning with those fishy
looking things mother never cooked,
but you still ate.
The days you drank too much
I cowered from your smell.
You never knew it hurt
to see your clear eyes go blurred,
to see your fingers fumble for a match
that never lit the dangling cigarette.

You never knew I wet my pillow
oftener than I had ever wet my bed.

Forgive me for the things I said.
Grown fifteen and above I thought
that wisdom lay in startling words.
In saying cad and bastard
a thousand times inside, and finding
substitutes in my pair of eyes,
I lied.

Wherever you are, will you
turn your index finger away?

I grant you divine power that it took
to live your kind of life,
both villain and hero of the piece.
Father, perhaps you lived too much.

And now I'm writing with my life.
The price of an inherited crutch.

The Earthworm's Story

I lost this last bit of shine
scraping along the way.
The crow pecked,
the ant bit,
and the gravel sneered underbelly.
The damp gone, the leaves fall
heavy as plates, and clatter.
Above the fly stalks the air.
It does not matter
if that's your foot over me.

from *Skies of Design*

Do Not Tell the Children

I cannot hold you in my hand for long
nor comfort you with vagrant lullabies.
Your nature is to stray into the dark realms
of the hidden trees.
Comfort comes from knowing the safe places
deep and separate, past the beaches
and the furious sea.
You balance mountains on your forehead
and pine trees on your finger tips.
Alone, you fight the night screeches
of the sleepless birds and build your defences
like the jackal in the silhouette
of the enormous hill.

I have nothing to offer you
but an eternity of lines around my throat.
Circles of time.
There is no comfort in growing old.
The old are too old. So I have frozen the moment.
The precious moment is frozen forever.

Do not tell the children ghost stories.
Tell them the truth about ghosts,
for they were born with them embedded
in their folds.

Skies of Design

For you M, I undid all my hopes.
I made no claims to knowing you.

As on a distant whimper the ear cannot focus,
on a disappearing star the eye cannot alight.

No longer can I grasp the shadows,
nor comprehend their urgent passing.
Memories repeat themselves.
Dreams perpetuate their myths.
Rivers contemplate their sources.

Once our hearts were full.
Moons of beginning.
Skies of design.
And every wish for truth
implied the perfunctory lie.

All power, now, I take away from you.
As from my father, my brothers,
the ones before you.

I shall bury you under the slipping sands
so that generations of memories
can rise upon you.
Rise over the distorted rainbow
into the suspended skies.

Doris

Gently touch the earth.
It locks your feet.
It locks your feeble heart
that's losing time.
No one calls you Doris any more.

For the first time
the firm earth trembles.
It opened and swallowed them
one by one. The ones you went
to school with, who later
served their husbands as you did.
Early mother, late widow.

Your sons have long dispersed
your daughters drag their feet.
You are no longer sure.
That early confidence and
stern hold on our ears
has broken into fear.
Fear of the dark
and fear that you might
wet your bed
and we'd hear about it.

No one calls you Doris any more
because they are dead.
Alive, are your granddaughters
and grandsons
pursuing the same ancient plague.
You would warn them,
but only brittle age rolls off your tongue.

Cat

You curl into your mouth.
Catscratch you fold
your claws inwards.
Cold world of purr and fur.
All plans are clandestine.
Night thief. Lover in the dark.
United silhouette on the roof top.
Careful confident master.

You start your climactic wail
growing in possibility
till it cracks the window pane
and pads off into the cool black.
Cat nap.

Bird Broken

Bird broken on a flying wing
you stumble on the air.
All night's spent in travelling
a wound upon the wind.

The strictures in your throat dissolve
rebuking all those private lies.
No one knows about the fractures
in the asphalt
only visible to those that fly.

Bird flying on a broken wing
soon your voice will break
and sing to some
dark, columnar mass.

Tight, light sheaf of feathers
angling to the earth.
To a resounding burial
of air and dirt.

Eunice de Souza

Born 1940. Eunice de Souza was educated in Bombay and the United States and received her Ph.D. from the University of Bombay with a thesis on 'The Critic in a Post-colonial Culture'. Her first book, *Fix*, was published in 1979, *Women in Dutch Painting* in 1988, *Ways of Belonging*, which was awarded a Poetry Book Society Recommendation, in 1990, and *Selected and New Poems* in 1994. She has written four books of folk-tales for children, and co-edited, with Adil Jussawalla, an anthology of Indian prose in English entitled *Statements*, in 1976. Some of the anthologies in which her work has been included are *Making for the Open: The Chatto Book of Post-Feminist Verse*, *The Virago Book of Love Poetry*, *The Faber Book of Vernacular Verse*, *The Virago Book of Wicked Verse*, and *The Oxford India Anthology of Twelve Modern Indian Poets*.

Several poets co-operated in the publication of *Fix*, Eunice de Souza's first book. Newground, the co-operative started by Melanie Silgardo, Raul D'Gama Rose and Santan Rodrigues published it, Arun Kolatkar designed the cover, A.D. Hope and Adil Jussawalla provided the blurbs, and Arvind Krishna Mehrotra, Saleem Peeradina, Kersey Katrak, and Jussawalla reviewed it.

With this auspicious start, it is not surprising that *Fix*, a hard-edged, somewhat violent book, has survived as the most distinctive of de Souza's books. For Veronica Brady, writing in the *Journal of Literature and Theology*,[1] many of the Catholic characters which appear in the poems are 'an embodiment of the complacency, the closed heart and mind which constitutes evil in de Souza's world because it entails the refusal of freedom, the "passion for the possible" . . . as distinct from the cultural religiosity she attacks here'. It is in this sense, Veronica Brady suggests, that de Souza's poetry can be called 'religious poetry'.[2] In addition, the sense of pain, loss, and the absence of God are central to de Souza's poetry.

1 ' "One Long Cry in the Dark"? The Poetry of Eunice de Souza', *Journal of Literature and Theology*, vol. 3, no. 1, March 1991, p. 113.

2 Ibid., p. 115.

Several members of de Souza's community saw *Fix* as a betrayal. Some of de Souza's students told her that the book had been denounced from the pulpit at St Peter's in Bandra. Adil Jussawalla assured her that if she continued the same way, she would soon be denounced at St Peter's in Rome.

For Arvind Krishna Mehrotra in *Twelve Modern Indian Poets*,[3] it is de Souza's 'microphoned ear' for speech patterns that is of special interest, especially the speech of some members of her community, which she renders without making them sound 'picturesque or "babu" '.[4]

Women in Dutch Painting is a 'softer' book than *Fix* and more varied in its landscapes and effects, though existential search, meshed with social concern, dominates. It is melancholy, witty, and even lyrical by turns. Much of it was written in England, far from the usual combat zones, and perhaps this accounts for the greater equanimity of the persona. The title poem sets the mood, evocative of the Dutch school of painting of which it speaks.

Ways of Belonging and *New and Selected Poems* are both volumes of selected poems, but each contains a section of new poems. *New and Selected Poems* has a detailed essay on the poet's work by Keith Fernandes who also edited the volume. Many of the new poems move nearer to de Souza's ideal of imagistic poetry which is both concentrated and resonant at the same time. De Souza's other ideal is the long, meditative 'Larkinsque' poem. For the moment, however, de Souza's poems continue to rely on the telling visual detail.

[3] Oxford University Press, Delhi, 1992, p. 114.
[4] Ibid.

from *Fix*

Catholic Mother

Francis X D'Souza
father of the year.
Here he is top left
the one smiling.
By the grace of God he says
we've had seven children
(in seven years).
We're One Big Happy Family
God Always Provides
India will Suffer for
her Wicked Ways
(these Hindu buggers got no ethics).

Pillar of the Church
says the parish priest
Lovely Catholic Family
says Mother Superior

The pillar's wife
says nothing.

Miss Louise

She dreamt of descending
curving staircases
ivory fan aflutter
of children in sailor suits
and organza dresses
till the dream rotted her innards
but no one knew:
innards weren't permitted
in her time.

Shaking her greying ringlets:
'My girl, I can't even
go to Church you know

I unsettle the priests
so completely. Only yesterday
that handsome Fr Hans was saying,
"Miss Louise, I feel an arrow
through my heart."
But no one will believe me
if I tell them. It's always
been the same. They'll say,
"Yes Louisa, we know, professors
loved you in your youth,
judges in your prime." '

For a Child, Not Clever

Once you thought it good
you came fifty-sixth in class
out of fifty-six children.
But Mummy, you said,
fifty-six is bigger than one.
Voices crackle and break
around you. Why do you provoke
your sisters? Why do you never
tell us about your tests?
To me, the cousin who visits
sometimes, you say, as if
explaining things: I'm not clever,
you see, that's why these things
keep happening.

You have pierced me with your pain
dunce dunce double d
Suddenly I see
how it's possible in Gethsamene
to say: I am the one you seek.
Let the rest go free.

40

Autobiographical

Right, now here it comes.
I killed my father when I was three.
I have muddled through several affairs
and always come out badly.
I've learned almost nothing from experience.
I head for the abyss with
monotonous regularity.

My enemies say I'm a critic because
really I'm writhing with envy
and anyway need to get married.

My friends say I'm not
entirely without talent.

Yes, I've tried suicide.
I tidied my clothes but
left no notes. I was surprised
to wake up in the morning.

One day my soul
stood outside me
watching me twitch
and grin and gibber
the skin tight
over my bones.

I thought the whole world
was trying to rip me up
cut me down go through me
with a razor blade.

Then I discovered
a cliché: that's what I wanted
to do to the world.

from *Women in Dutch Painting*

Pilgrim

I

The hills crawl with convoys.
Slow lights wind round
and down the dark ridges
to yet another
termite city.

The red god rock
watches all that passes.
He spoke once.
The blood-red boulders
are his witness.

God rock, I'm a pilgrim.
Tell me —
Where does the heart find rest?

II

There's a continent moving
under my feet, god rock.
In a million years
it will swallow the seas,
spew out mountains,
reduce this land
to a handful of gravel.

Give us a sign, god rock.

A city burns.

III

God Rock's Passion

God rock plunged into
the belly of the earth, molten.

Heaved off,
goat pellet seed.

Primeval slob.

The Road

As we came out of the church
into the sunlight
a row of small girls
in first communion dresses
I felt the occasion demanded
lofty thoughts.

I remember
only my grandmother
smiling at me.

They said
now she wears lipstick
now she is a Bombay girl
they said, your mother is lonely.
Nobody said, even the young must live.

In school
I clutched Sister Flora's skirt
and cried for my mother
who taught across the road.
Sister Flora is dead.
The school is still standing.
I am still learning
to cross the road.

from *Ways of Belonging*

Bequest

In every Catholic home there's a picture
of Christ holding his bleeding heart
in his hand.
I used to think, ugh.

43

The only person with whom
I have not exchanged confidences
is my hairdresser.

Some recommend stern standards
others say float along.
He says, take it as it comes,
meaning, of course, as he hands it out.

I wish I could be a
Wise Woman
smiling endlessly, vacuously
like a plastic flower,
saying Child, learn from me.

It's time to perform an act of charity
to myself,
bequeath the heart, like a
spare kidney —
preferably to an enemy.

from *Selected and New Poems*

Landscape

I

M. assures me she'll be back
to fling my ashes in the local creek.
(We're short on sacred rivers here).

The pungent air will suit my soul:
It will find its place among
the plastic carrier bags and rags that float upstream
or is it downstream.
One can never tell.
The sea sends everything reeling back.
The trees go under.

44

II

We push so much under the carpet —
the carpet's now a landscape.
A worm embedded in each tuft
There's a forest moving.

Everybody smiles
and smiles.

III

The crows will never learn
there is garbage enough for everyone:
the mouths of the young are raw red,
soundless.

The egret alights on the topmost branch.
Not a leaf is disturbed.
On all sides the ocean.

IV

stretch marks of the city

Look the other way:
There are dhows there
mud banks
white horses for desert kingdoms.

an old monkey coughs in a tree

the young sense food
begin their walk up the hill
slow sure unceasing

we lock the windows
bar the doors

the sun burns through the walls

Outside Jaisalmer

I

The sea receded. The dunes remember.
Trees have turned quietly to stone.

I watch two men bend intently
over a pawnbroker's scales

and think of you:

Walled city. Dead kings.
The tarred road melts where we stand.

II

Sixty miles from the border
stories:
the general on the other side
doesn't want war, he wants to
cultivate his poppy fields.

We're here to watch the sun set.
Birds fly in formation, and jets.

III

The life of the hero on the scabbard of a sword.
Faces in profile, erect penis in profile,
the colours raw, the rug in detail.
The milk he's washed in has turned a little sour.
Her hand touches her veil.
He looks into her eyes
she looks into his.
Behind the lattice work the waiting women
cry oh and stroke their breasts.

IV

We clatter over five river beds
broad, sweeping, dry
tour potters' weavers' villages
and Kuldera, deserted in protest
against a greedy king.

46

An old man brings out a few fossils
and says, 'Once there was a sea,'
(a hundred and eighty million years ago
but he doesn't know that).

The children say Hello
and look at my shoes.

It's Time to Find a Place

It's time to find a place
to be silent with each other.
I have prattled endlessly
in staff-rooms, corridors, restaurants.
When you're not around
I carry on conversations in my head.
Even this poem
has forty-eight words too many.

Imtiaz Dharker

Born 1954 in Lahore. Imtiaz Dharkar was raised and educated in Britain, and now lives in India. She was Consulting Poetry Editor for *Debonair* from 1975 to 1985. She is a documentary film-maker; one of her documentaries won the Silver Lotus Award for the best short film in 1980. She is also an artist who has exhibited here and abroad. Her first book, *Purdah*,[1] was published in 1989, and her second, *Postcards from god*,[2] in 1994.

Imtiaz Dharker's first book, *Purdah*, contains a two-part poem called 'Outline' in which she describes a sculptor working at creating a human body. In the first part, the sculptor deliberately stops at the moment of high tension, when the figure will be revealed at its most intriguing. In the second, unconscious forces take over when the artist tries to restrict the figure, and the end-product is more interesting than it would have been in its more confined state.

In 'Battle-line', one of the better poems in *Purdah*, Imtiaz Dharker achieves this tension in evoking the conflicts between man and woman, who can either be lovers or husband and wife. The poem reveals an imaginative understanding of the states of mind of both protagonists. In contrast, the poems about women in Purdah II[3] (purdah not just as concealing garment but as state of mind) tend to be flattened out by the overriding emotion of compassion. Some of the women do 'break cover', as the speaker advises, and find 'another man', or an 'English boy / who was going to set you free'. But all attempts at escape end with the women on their knees. For immigrant women in England, there is the further burden of hostility. One or two of these women are given names: 'Naseem', or 'Saleema of the swan neck'. The speaker says, 'I can see behind their veils, and before they speak / I know their tongues, thick / with the burr of Birmingham or

---

[1] Oxford University Press, Delhi, 1989.
[2] Viking, Delhi, 1994.
[3] *Purdah*, pp. 5–10.

Leeds'. It's a pity that in this poem, and others, one does not actually hear these voices. What one hears is the speaker's voice expressing her compassion, and the many different women merge into one — somewhat cardboardish — object. The feel for the vitalizing detail revealed in 'Battle-line', the sense of the nitty-gritty of the women's lives is missing. This is a recurrent problem with poems about an oppressed group. The heart is certainly in the right place, but more than that is required for a poem to come alive.

Postcards from god is a stronger book, not because the poet had first-hand information about God, but because the concept of God is a kind of blank space into which anything can be read. In this book, God contemplates with dismay, the creation for which he is held accountable, and the strange uses to which his name is put in religious antagonisms. The strongest poem in the book, however, is 'Living Space', which catches exactly the ramshackle quality of life in this country, and the spirit of survival that so often and so mysteriously accompanies it.

from *Purdah*

Purdah I

One day they said
she was old enough to learn some shame.
She found it came quite naturally.

Purdah is a kind of safety.
The body finds a place to hide.
The cloth fans out against the skin
much like the earth that falls
on coffins after they put the dead men in.

People she has known
stand up, sit down as they have always done.
But they make different angles
in the light, their eyes aslant,
a little sly.

She half-remembers things
from someone else's life,
perhaps from yours, or mine —
carefully carrying what we do not own:
between the thighs, a sense of sin.

We sit still, letting the cloth grow
a little closer to our skin.
A light filters inward
through our bodies' walls.
Voices speak inside us,
echoing in the spaces we have just left.

She stands outside herself,
sometimes in all four corners of a room.
Wherever she goes, she is always
inching past herself,
as if she were a clod of earth,
and the roots as well,
scratching for a hold
between the first and second rib.

Passing constantly out of her own hands
into the corner of someone else's eyes . . .
while doors keep opening
inward and again
inward.

Battle-line

Did you expect dignity?

All you see is bodies
crumpled carelessly, and thrown
away.
The arms and legs are never arranged
heroically.

It's the same with lovers
after the battle-lines are drawn:
combatants thrown
into something they have not
had time to understand.
And in the end, just
a reflex turning away
when there is nothing, really,
left to say;

when the body becomes a territory
shifting across uneasy sheets;

when you retreat behind
the borderline of skin.

Turning, turning,
barbed wire sinking in.

These two countries lie
hunched against each other
distrustful lovers
who have fought bitterly
and turned their backs;
but in sleep, drifted slowly
in, moulding themselves
around the cracks

to fit together,
whole again; at peace.

Forgetful of hostilities
until, in the quiet dawn,
the next attack.

Checkpoint:
The place in the throat
where words are halted,
not allowed to pass,
where questions form
and are not asked.

Checkpoint:
The space on the skin
that the other cannot touch;
where you are the guard
at every post
holding a deadly host
of secrets in.

Checkpoint:
Another country. You.
Your skin the bright, sharp line
that I must travel to.

I watch his back,
and from my distance map
its breadth and strength.

His muscles tense.
His body tightens
into a posture of defence.

He goes out, comes in.
His movements are angles
sharp enough to slice my skin.

He cuts across the room —
his territory. I watch
the cautious way he turns his head.

52

He throws back the sheet. At last
his eyes meet mine.

Together,
we have reached the battle-line.

Having come home,
all you can do is leave.

Spaces become too small.
Doors and windows begin
to hold your breath.
Floors shift underfoot, you bruise yourself
against a sudden wall.

You come into a room;
strangers haggle over trivial things —
a grey hair curls in a comb.
Someone tugs sadly at your sleeve.

But no one screams.

Because, leaving home,
you call yourself free.

Because, behind you,
barbed wire grows
where you once
had planted a tree.

from *Postcards from god*

Words Find Mouths

Things were meant to flow
one from another.
They were meant to grow
into one another; to know
the taste and feel of
being part of one vast whole.

All that stopped
when words found mouths,
when tongues wagged their way
into minds,
and each object shrank, suddenly,
to fit its own precise outline.

You could say
that was when the trouble started:

When things stepped into the cage
of a purpose I must have had
somewhere in my mind.

Living Space

There are just not enough
straight lines. That
is the problem.
Nothing is flat
or parallel. Beams
balance crookedly on supports
thrust off the vertical.
Nails clutch at open seams.
The whole structure leans dangerously
towards the miraculous.

Into this rough frame,
someone has squeezed
a living space

and even dared to place
these eggs in a wire basket,
fragile curves of white
hung out over the dark edge
of a slanted universe,
gathering the light
into themselves,
as if they were
the bright, thin walls of faith.

54

Eggplant

Impossible to hold,
you have to cradle it,
let it slide against your cheek.

If this could speak,
this eggplant,
it would have the voice
of a plump child-god,
purple-blue and sleek
with happiness,
full of milk,
ready to sleep.

Namesake

Adam, your namesake lives
in Dharavi, ten years old. He
has never faced the angels, survives
with pigs that root
outside the door,
gets up at four,
follows his mother to the hotel
where he helps her cut
the meat and vegetables, washes
it all well, watches
the cooking pots over the stove
and waits, his eyelids drooping,
while behind the wall she sells herself
as often as she can before
they have to hurry home.

He very rarely runs
shrieking with other rain-
splashed children
down the sky-paved lane.

He never turns to look at you.
He has no memory
of the Garden, paradise water
or the Tree.

But if he did, Adam, he
would not think to blame you
or even me
for the wrath that has been visited,
inexplicably, on him.

Reflected in sheets of water
at his back
stand the avenging angels
he will never see.

8 January 1993

The bolt bangs in.
A match is struck and thrown.
The burning has begun.

Afterwards
the bodies are removed
one by one.

And this is left:
blackened saris, trousers, petticoats,
the shell of a television set,
a tin box of bangles
and face cream,
a blistered cupboard
like a looted face
that opened its mouth

in a scream
that never found an end.

The List

Sudden impact.
The city flies apart.

Bits of high-rise apartments,
scraps of slums,
all kinds of shops
empty themselves into the sky.

Loaves of bread explode from bakeries.
Fishes catapult out of the sea.
Buses, suburban trains and taxis
spit out their load.
Things lose their names.

Pieces of wreckage rise
in a slow-motion symmetry.

This must be how war feels:
When ordinary things lose
their sense of gravity.

Old men settle deeper
in their chairs
like sacred stones.
Death is elsewhere.

And then, the last absurdity.
The banging at the door.

You expect more —
perhaps jack-booted men,
not this small crowd
of children, fists
clamped round match-boxes,
sticks and ball-point pens,
and the final weapon:
The list,
to be read aloud.

Your name is there.
It settles on you like a shroud.

57

Minority

I was born a foreigner.
I carried on from there
to become a foreigner everywhere
I went, even in the place
planted with my relatives,
six-foot tubers sprouting roots,
their fingers and faces pushing up
new shoots of maize and sugar cane.

All kinds of places and groups
of people who have an admirable
history would, almost certainly,
distance themselves from me.

I don't fit,
like a clumsily-translated poem;

like food cooked in milk of coconut
where you expected ghee or cream,
the unexpected aftertaste
of cardamom or neem.

There's always that point where
the language flips
into an unfamiliar taste;
where words tumble over
a cunning tripwire on the tongue;
where the frame slips,
the reception of an image
not quite tuned, ghost-outlined,
that signals, in their midst,
an alien.

And so I scratch, scratch
through the night, at this
growing scab of black on white.
Everyone has the right
to infiltrate a piece of paper.
A page doesn't fight back.
And, who knows, these lines

may scratch their way
into your head —
through all the chatter of community,
family, clattering spoons,
children being fed —
immigrate into your bed,
squat in your home,
and in a corner, eat your bread,

until, one day, you meet
the stranger sidling down your street,
realize you know the face
simplified to bone,
look into its outcast eyes
and recognize it as your own.

Smita Agarwal

Born 1958. Smita Agarwal teaches at the University of Allahabad where she worked for her Ph.D. on Sylvia Plath. She is a vocal artist for All India Radio. Though she has been publishing poems for twenty years she has not yet published a book. The poems included here are from her unpublished manuscript 'Glitch'. She also publishes stories for children.

In a short piece on poetry written for *The Times of India*, Smita Agarwal says that 'a poem performs a civilizing function, answering not only a human need for emotional expression but for rational control as well'. Poetry does this by resolving 'warring forces', and she goes on to discuss the ways in which the poetry of Meerabai, Sylvia Plath and Emily Dickinson finds ways to explore and control these forces. Through this exploration and control, both poet and reader find new ways of understanding themselves and life.

Again, reviews that Smita Agarwal has written about the work of poets in India suggest an interest in T.S. Eliot's theory of impersonality. She says, for instance, that Imtiaz Dharker's second book *Postcards from god* 'registers a growth, a fanning out of consciousness from the personal to the social . . . ' Smita Agarwal is frequently concerned with pain, but, in the tradition of impersonality it is expressed through the dramatized consciousness of other people, or other forms of life. The speaker in 'The Salesman', for instance, is aware of the reception he is likely to get and is hypersensitive about every move and sound he makes. The speaker in 'The Drake' wonders on one of his sojourns: 'Why is it I / Tire, feel old and abject? Should I / Give up migrations, settle down to rest?'

Smita Agarwal also writes poems that begin with observations of nature, and then go on to an insight about a person or situation, personal or social. Among the poems not included, the rain, 'tattooing on the roof' in 'Monsoon Cantata' increases in violence till it brings in its wake 'communal / Conflagrations, scams, arms deals, a tribal / Woman gang-raped, mute deaths in custody/India in the nineteen nineties'. In 'Alphabets of Nature', the speaker's small son examines flowers and plants, pulls some apart, flings them away. The speaker wonders what the child will be like when he is a man, and married. 'I can see him, years later, examining / A body. Son, will you by chance / Recollect the insular glory of your Father / Inviolate in his separate bedroom / The day you tire of your wife?'

'The Lie of the Land: A Letter to Chatwin' turns topography into a meditation on perspectives, misreadings, miscalculations in one's life. 'The Map' examines a 'smallish piece of paper' on which the map is drawn in bright colours, and turns it into a voyage of discovery, full of surprises and mysteries.

In other words, Smita Agarwal's poems perform that civilizing function she has commented on in her discussions of poets, and reveal, at every turn, 'a self acutely aware of life'. Her achievement is all the more remarkable when one considers the fact that she is writing, as she says, 'essentially in isolation', and is 'primarily self-taught'. Academic life is vitiated by 'provincial vigilantism' and 'homicidal gossip'. In contrast, she adds, it is 'middle-class lawyers, judges, businessmen and their wives [who] are responsive and encouraging, though most times they don't understand much of what you write. A woman is trying to come into her own. They appreciate and encourage that'.

from unpublished ms 'Glitch'

The Lie of the Land: A Letter to Chatwin

If I were to set stock
In your words Bruce,
If, as you deduce,
Man is migratory,
May be I'd venture to say
That land is meant
For aerial viewing.

Upright, I'm uptight; I hardly
Ever range beyond my nose. Avian,
On my belly, I'd at least see
The ditches, gullies, promontories,
Foot-wide streams cutting deep
Into cartilage and bone of soil,
Camouflaged by thickets, thick as hair.
Land never fails to surprise.
What I perceive as a stable
Patch of green may very well
Decline to bear dead weight,
And instead, have my legs flail
In a void. Or, as I brace myself
For a mile of arduous ascent, the
Mountain may decide to become the
Shoulder of a hill; there, where I'd
Envisaged an apex, may lie a
Plateau-like ridge; a pine-encrusted
Slope may give me the slip
And have me come down hard —
Down to the very rock-bottom.

All muscle and bone, my legs feel
Responsible for most of my bad-hair
Days. If I were a creepy-crawly,
Or an airy-fairy, I'd at least
Stick to instincts; never dare;

Nor feel piqued at the bamboo's
Jointed stilts able to
Wave to the sun, bow to the wind. —

The Salesman

Making sure there's no one around
I confront the first, lift my right
Leg high, miss the mark, hear in the
Silent stairwell the flat sound of
A shoed foot striking stone; in my
Mouth the well known, indefinable
Taste of a tap run dry.
Right angled, poker-face perfect

Stairs, sentinelled by a set of
Walls speeding along, taken by
Surprise at each fall and rise,
Thrown completely out of gear
At every fleshed out corner.
What am I doing here? My finger
On a bell, *Bing-bong*. The cut-out
Of a door introducing a

Space, framing a face; the initial,
Quizzical look hardening into a
Stare; a disembodied
Syllable *Yes?* drilling a hole
At a certain place: I visualize
The contortions of a half-loose
Paper poster on a wall,
Madly flapping in the wind.

The Planetoid

It drifts slowly, dreaming. This is
No straight and narrow path but an
Orbit with no signposts at the
Bends. The planetoid senses it —

A shower of meteorites awaits it.
At first a rock fragment or two.
Later, full-scale bombardment that
Might take in its wake a portion
Of its crust. The planetoid is
Accustomed to these astroblemes.
What it fears is plate tectonics.
Words shifting then falling into
Place but not without having first
Created gaps, fissures, chasms,
Other kinds of yawning space. The
Planetoid wishes to avoid
Disfigurement. But it cannot
Veer out of a predestined course.

Daywatch in the Scriptorium

The guests have departed.
The raging fever gone.
This blank page beckons me
To give it something of myself.

Oak leaves turn in the wind,
Moss-green on silver. The
Mesh of needles on a coniferous
Branch, flat as a palm, strains
The sunlight. Behind a hill, it
Seems as if an invisible Indian
Chief has hunkered down to puff
Out spreading clouds of peace.
A rufous-throated nuthatch
Is disappointed. The apples
Are small, hard and green.
It flies away boring through
Haze and rows of hills.

Fair, weather, like a leafed twig
Suddenly landing at my feet,
Don't welsh on me. Green lion*
Day in June, live on in memory.

The Word-worker
(For Jeanette Winterson)

My eyes lick them off the page;
I chew them, suck the juices,
Let the flavours seep in. I am
The dreamer; words, the cocoon
I knit. Fixed for ever in the
Slim gap between alphabets
I am the saboteur, the hit-man.
Words scurry down dark lanes
Or brightly lit streets. I rip
Off masks, bequeath new skin,
Dragoon words into birthing
Faces never before born.

A Grass Widow's Prayer

Tall hill speckled with pine;
The air scented. Again I
Undertake the annual ascent up
The spiralling way to your temple.
It is *Navaratra*. The goddess is
A decked out bride. I go to
Offer her a red scarf trimmed
With gold lace. Just-married girls spill
Out of taxis and buses. They're on
Their first visit to *Surkhanda*
With their spouses. The lucky ones

* Green lion: A spirit of great transmuting power supposed to be produced by
certain processes in alchemy; sometimes identified with the philosophical mer-
cury (OED).

Shall meet their kin and shop
At the fair. Meanwhile, I shall wind
A red and gold thread round the peepul;
Tie tiny brass bells to its outstretched
Arms; bells that shall peal out my
Prayers to the unseen gods that look
Askance at my bare wrists, my forehead clear
Of the sacramental dot, the parting in my hair
A quiet, empty street. *Devi-Ma*, I come
To deepen your red with my
Absence of colour. Keep him safe;
He who is alone at his outpost
Battling shadows and sounds.
May he win the war he set out for.

Mediatrix

1

A man in love is in love with his own shadow,
a shadow that must follow and fit his notion
of love. He's in love neither with a contour,
nor a mind, but simply with an idea of himself.
Circling the flame he'll try to coincide
with his shadow till a woman in love with
a man in love lets him see and sets him free.

2

Never hunt him down.
Do not put words into
his mouth. Do not remind him
of his mother. Be patient, stand
aloof. Let hunger, loneliness and a
pelting rain leave him stranded under your roof.

'Our foster-nurse of nature is repose'

Lying in bed on a pure-white sheet, the
air-conditioner whirring, I stare at the
strip light and when the eyes smart
I turn and it seems, for the first time,
I consider your features.

Eyelashes like an aunt's, inked and curled;
mouth-pout petulant, the shape of your limbs
like your father's. Not even your temper
matches mine.

Wheat-gold child, sleeping.
You assure me I belong to
the land of *Karma*. Having performed my
duty why should I wish that my shadow,
like a stamp, should brand you?

What gesture of atonement can I make?
You whom I've flogged in dreams each
time you upset an apple-cart with a
sneeze or fever?

Let me clear this room of frost and fire.
Shoo away clamour, turn out the light that
drills through your lids. What can I give you,
before the world claims you, but
these few hours of uninterrupted sleep?

Discord

She sits on the rattan chair,
I, opposite her, on the sofa.
Between us, on the covered floor,
our two boys play war games.
Floral arrangements on the
ersatz Persian rug unroll
before my eyes; her rigid spine,
the way she concentrates

on her needlepoint. Her
secret pain comes gushing
out. Unable to do or say anything
I explore inter-stellar space
in a bid to fix the design.
They've been at it again
like two crossed knives, husband and wife.

Sujata Bhatt

Born 1956. Sujata Bhatt was educated in the USA where her
scientist father had settled and now lives in Germany. She has
published three books of poems, *Brunizem* (1988) which won the
Commonwealth Poetry Prize for the Asia Section, *Monkey Shadows*
(1991) which won a Poetry Book Society Recommendation, and
The Stinking Rose (1994). She has also translated Gujarati poetry
into English.

Biographical notes and blurbs tend to stress Sujata Bhatt's 'multi-
culturalism'. Ranjana Ash, for instance, tells us that Sujata Bhatt
writes of 'the anguish of immigrants when they start to lose their
first language', and she comments approvingly on the poet's
attempt to use Gujarati lines interspersed with English ones 'for
onomatopoeic effect, and because for her certain subjects cannot
be described in English'.[1]

Looking through the now copious material, essays, poems,
memoirs, on the multicultural experience, one finds words such
as 'anguish', and 'exile' appearing fairly frequently. The ongoing
debates between those who see themselves as 'assimilated' and
those who think of assimilation as betrayal of one's roots, tend
to be as polemical as the now-dated debates between nativists and
writers in English in India used to be. So bitter is the feeling
against Bharati Mukherjee's intention of seeing herself in the
tradition of other American writers, and against Vikram Seth's
The Golden Gate because it contains 'not a clue of his Indianness',
that Feroza Jussawalla, writing in *The Massachusetts Review*[2] finds
it possible, in all seriousness, to quote one of Raja Rao's more
foolish statements against these writers as proof of his Indianness.
Raja Rao writes: 'I have often recited Kalidasa to the Seine and
she seemed to remember.'

[1] Ian Hamilton (ed.), *The Oxford Companion to Twentieth Century Poetry in English*,
Oxford University Press, Oxford, 1994, p. 45.

[2] 'Chiffon Saris: The Plight of South Asian Immigrants in the New World', *The
Massachusetts Review*, Winter 1988–9. Reference to Bharati Mukherjee, p. 591, to
Vikram Seth, p. 592, to Raja Rao, p. 593.

There is no evidence in Feroza Jussawalla's essay to suggest that she is aware that what finally counts is the quality of the craftsmanship. A string of multicultural place names does not automatically create a resonant poem. Poems of this kind, in fact, often rely on an identity buzz or political correctness to do their work for them. And if collections of diaspora writing are anything to go by, interspersing English lines with those from the author's first language is an increasingly popular device, a style which is said to have originated with two Hispanic women writers, Cherri Moraga and Gloria Anzaldua.

Sujata Bhatt's 'Search for My Tongue' in *Brunizem* is an eight-page poem using Gujarati lines, followed by the same in Roman script, followed by a translation in English. These devices are used in all three books. Sometimes there is Gujarati in the title along with the English title, and some poems use a few Gujarati words. Others use German, Gujarati and English, and one uses Sanskrit. Because of the extensive use of Gujarati, I requested a colleague, Dr Shefali Balsari-Shah to comment on the bilingualism of the poems. She writes:

Sujata Bhatt's experiments in bi-lingual poetry explore the conflict of the self divided between different cultures. While some of the poems which make extensive use of Gujarati are elaborately wrought and can occasionally seduce the bi-lingual reader into easy, instant empathy, they don't necessarily work as good poetry.

At the most obvious level the Gujarati sections serve to shut out rather than include the general reader for whom presumably the poems are written. One could of course argue that the incomprehensibility is a deliberate part of the poet's design to draw the reader into her own sense of otherness in order to experience a predicament which allows only a fragmented or peripheral existence. But once she has established the feeling and the novelty of its expression has waned, how is it developed?

At the beginning of 'Search for My Tongue', the Gujarati sentences are translated quite literally into English. As the poem progresses the Gujarati lines remain flat, prosaic and closed, while the English sentences that follow become longer and richer, spinning off associations and graphically building on them so that they work quite independently of the Gujarati original.

The use of Gujarati is perhaps most extraneous in 'A Different Way to Dance'.[3] While being driven through New England the poet's mother suddenly exclaims *aray paylo hathi jai*. The sight of a huge elephant

[3] *Monkey Shadows*, Penguin India, 1993, p. 33.

careening down an American highway in a truck may indeed be ludic-rous, but the use of Gujarati hardly seems necessary to create this tone.

The mother-tongue–foreign language controversy has several aspects which are open to debate. One rather facile assumption is that the Indian self can be truly defined only in purely Indian terms whether of ethos, myth or language; its corollary is that while thinking may occur in any language, all genuine feeling can only be in the mother-tongue. But Sujata Bhatt's poetry works against this ideology. Her Gujarati is plodding, unremarkable, or simply banal, nowhere conveying the inef-fable quality that eludes translation, while her poetic voice in English can be sensitive, vivid and evocative. Consequently, the Gujarati ele-ments seem unconvincing, and can best be viewed as self-indulgence or a fashionable gimmick.

Yet 'Search for My Tongue', clumsy and contrived though it is, is the only one of Sujata Bhatt's poems published in a US diaspora anthology, *Our Feet Walk the Sky* (1993).[4]

The poems included here represent the poet at her unforced best. In 'The Peacock' for instance, she catches the singularity of the bird, its miraculous beauty, and the sense of stillness one feels in the presence of such beauty. 'For Paula Modersohn-Becker' captures the fascination the speaker feels for a painting and a painter who seems to understand her feelings so well that she can imagine 'arguing with you about whether to put garlic in the soup'. 'White Asparagus' is the only erotic poem in Sujata Bhatt's collections that works, and the only successful erotic poem in Indian writing in English. The poet moves again between object and subjective feelings in ways that catch both the singularity of the object and the fascination it inspires.

Sujata Bhatt's third book, *The Stinking Rose*, is a very weak one, and bears the mark of poems written with a programme in mind. Twenty-five poems are about garlic lore. The lore is interesting, the poems are not. To the problem of prosiness in her earlier books, especially in the long narrative poems, she adds the problem of an extensive use of inane rhetorical questions. For instance, 'Instructions to the Artist' begins, 'How can I know what I want?' and ends, 'But how about the human figure? /

---

[4] Edited by The Women of South Asian Descent Collective, Aunt Lute Books, San Francisco, 1993.

Can you include it somehow with the garlic and the roses / I don't mean just any human figure . . . '[5]

The fact that Sujata Bhatt's first book contains some viable poems and her third book none suggests that she should perhaps forget about unique selling points and go on doing what she does well until she can find a way to handle experiment more convincingly.

5 *Carcanet*, Manchester, 1995, p. 61.

from *Brunizem*

The Peacock

His loud sharp call
seems to come from nowhere.
Then, a flash of turquoise
        in the pipal tree.
The slender neck arched away from you
        as he descends,
and as he darts away, a glimpse
        of the very end of his tail.

I was told
that you have to sit in the veranda
                and read a book,
preferably one of your favourites
        with great concentration.
The moment you begin to live
inside the book
a blue shadow will fall over you.
The wind will change direction,
the steady hum of bees
in the bushes nearby
will stop.
The cat will awaken and stretch.
Something has broken your attention;
and if you look up in time
you might see the peacock
turning away as he gathers in his tail
to shut those dark glowing eyes,
violet fringed with golden amber.
It is the tail that has to blink
for eyes that are always open.

For Paula Modersohn-Becker
(1876–1907)

The way I returned again and again to your self-portrait with
     blue irises
made the guards uneasy.

The way I turned away from your self-portrait with blue irises
made the guards uneasy.

Was it the blue irises floating around your face, was it
your brown eyes illuminated by something in the blue irises?

How could you know, how could you feel all this
that I know and feel about blue iris?

I was on the top floor with other paintings, other painters,
but unable to concentrate on them because
already I could hear the tone of voice your brown eyes would
     require.

So I rushed back down to be with you.

The look that passed between us must have lasted
a long time because I could smell the light
from the irises falling across your face.

The look that passed between us was full
of understanding so I could imagine living with you
and arguing with you about whether to put garlic in the soup.

I stared at the blue irises but in my throat
there was the pungent fresh bitterness of watercress.

When I finally left you I noticed three guards following me.

By the time I got home I was furious at them
for witnessing all this.

The Women of Leh are such —
for Jürgen Dierking

The women of Leh are such —
that one night over there, some 3,600 metres
high, not far from Tibet,
where the Zanskar glitters all day,
and at night, the stars, not to be outdone,
seem to grow larger, let themselves sink down closer
to the mountains — while the moon always disappears
by midnight, cut off by the horizon,
always on the other side
of some huge rock — one night
in that place I dreamt
and I saw Gertrude Stein selling
horseradishes and carrots. There was no mistaking
those shoulders — but she fit in so well
with her looking-straight-at-you eyes.
And yet, even the traditional
Ladakhi hat she wore could not disguise
her face. She said *jooley* to my *jooley*
with the others, all lined up along the main street —
she slapped the head of a hungry
rowdily exploring *dzo*
and I walked back, several times, back and forth,
pretending I couldn't decide what to buy.
Then she turned aside to talk with the tomato seller,
still keeping an eye on the *dzo* — it was hard to believe
but there was no mistaking that poise.

A Different History

Great Pan is not dead;
he simply emigrated
            to India.
Here, the gods roam freely,
disguised as snakes or monkeys;
every tree is sacred
and it is a sin

to be rude to a book.
It is a sin to shove a book aside
                with your foot,
a sin to slam books down
                hard on a table,
a sin to toss one carelessly
                across a room.
You must learn how to turn the pages gently
without disturbing Sarasvati,*
without offending the tree
from whose wood the paper was made.

2

Which language
has not been the oppressor's tongue?
Which language
truly meant to murder someone?
And how does it happen
that after the torture,
after the soul has been cropped
with a long scythe swooping out
of the conqueror's face —
the unborn grandchildren
grow to love that strange language.

Something for Plato

He holds out his lips,
this wreck of a rhinoceros:
dried-up gravel skin, limping with a crooked spine —
but who knows, maybe he's happy
kept like this in the Delhi zoo. Here he walks
like a fat man in a crisp red sports jacket
who doesn't think of himself as fat — he's so pleased
with the virile cut of his new sports jacket . . .

---

* Sarasvati: the goddess of knowledge. She presides over all the fine arts and is
worshipped in libraries.

Flabby cracked lips
shudder open, showing us a sharp triangular
smiling tongue. He keeps lifting up
those thick scabby rough lips, wobbling
with such a tender gesture,
an emotion so strong
the lines around his neck are suddenly delicate —
so graceful — he could be a young flamingo, a weeping willow
leaving no doubt
that he wants to be caressed. There's plenty
of grass around him
but he won't have it, he wants
to be hand-fed, wants his forehead stroked.
He'll put up with having his horn pulled at,
pretend his head can be jerked around
by the scrawny schoolboys — as long as they feed him,
the tips of their fingers arousing and soothing his mouth.

Iris

Her hand sweeps over the rough grained paper,
then, with a wet sponge, again.
A drop of black is washed grey,
cloudy as warm breath fogging cool glass.
She feels she must make the best of it,
she must get the colour of the stone wall,
of the mist settling around twisted birch trees.
Her eye doesn't miss the rabbit crouched,
a tuft of fog in the tall grass.
Nothing to stop the grey sky from merging into stones,
or the stone walls from trailing off into sky.
But closer, a single iris stands fully opened:
dark wrinkled petals, rain-moist,
the tall slender stalk sways, her hand follows.
Today, even the green is tinged with grey,
the stone's shadow lies heavy over the curling petals
but there's time enough, she'll wait,
study the lopsided shape.

The outer green sepals once enclosing the bud
lie shrivelled: empty shells spiralling
right beneath the petals.
As she stares the sun comes out.
And the largest petal flushes
deep deep violet.
A violet so intense it's almost black.
The others tremble indigo, reveal
paler blue undersides.
Thin red veins running into yellow orange rills,
yellow flows down the green stem.
Her hand moves swiftly from palette to paper,
paper to palette, the delicate brush
swoops down, sweeps up,
moves the way a bird builds its nest.
An instant and the sun is gone.
Grey-ash-soft-shadows fall again.
But she can close her eyes and see
red-orange veins, the yellow
swept with green throbbing towards blue,
and deep inside she feels
indigo pulsing to violet.

from *Monkey Shadows*

White Asparagus

Who speaks of the strong currents
streaming through the legs, the breasts
of a pregnant woman
in her fourth month?

She's young, this is her first time,
she's slim and the nausea has gone.
Her belly's just starting to get rounder
her breasts itch all day,

and she's surprised that what she wants
is *him*
            inside her again.

78

Oh come like a horse, she wants to say,
move like a dog, a wolf,
         become a suckling lion-cub —

Come here, and here, and here —
but swim fast and don't stop.

Who speaks of the green coconut uterus
the muscles sliding, a deeper undertow
and the green coconut milk that seals
her well, yet flows so she is wet
from his softest touch?

Who understands the logic
behind this desire?

Who speaks of the rushing tide
         that awakens
her slowly increasing blood — ?
And the hunger
         raw obsessions beginning
with the shape of asparagus:
sun-deprived white and purple-shadow-veined,
she buys three kilos
of the fat ones, thicker than anyone's fingers,
she strokes the silky heads,
some are so jauntily capped . . .
         even the smell pulls her in —

Kankaria Lake

Sometimes the nine-year-old boy
finds it difficult
to believe this is water.

It is more like skin;
a reptile's skin —
wrinkled and rough as a crocodile's
         and green.

Bacterial green, decomposed
green — opaque and dull.

As if the lake
were a giant crocodile
he couldn't see the ends of.

Kankaria Lake is on the way
to the Ahmedabad Zoo.
Sundays he always walks across
the bridge over the lake.

In the distance he can see
a small park bordered
      by the water — dry grass
struggles to grow against the scummy lake.
The park seems always deserted.

Sometimes a gardener
or a homeless man
or a wandering storyteller
would fall asleep on the grass
      too close to the lake —
and soon enough the newspapers
would report about how
the crocodiles had devoured
yet another careless man.

The boy thinks he would like to witness
      such an event.

But then, would he try
      to save the man?

He's not sure.

Or would he just watch
to see how a crocodile eats?

Would the man's legs go first
      or the arms
      or the stomach?

The boy imagines the lake
overpopulated with crocodiles
who never have enough to eat —
for he doesn't believe any fish
could live in such water.

There are hardly any trees
near the lake; no friendly monkeys
who would throw fruits down
to the crocodiles, as they do
        in one old story . . .

Kankaria Lake had also become
the most popular place
for suicides — That was a fact
which felt more like science-fiction
        to him.

On those Sunday afternoon
        family outings
he stops
in the middle of the bridge
and leans out
        towards the lake,
now and then sticking his legs out
through the railing
hoping at least one crocodile
will surface,
        raise its head.

But no.
Nothing ever happens.
Sometimes the wind pokes
the lake, making murky ripples.
But the crocodiles prefer
to remain hidden below.
How do they breathe?
        He worries.

In the end he was
always marched off
disappointed to the zoo
where he faced sullen animals
sometimes crouched far away
in the darkest part of the cage,
frightened in
        their festering skins.

Charmayne D'Souza

Born 1955. D'Souza read for an M.A. in English Literature at the University of Bombay, and an M.A. in Counselling at Northern State College, USA. She won three prizes for poetry in the USA: the Aberdeen (South Dakota) Arts Council Prize in 1985 and 1986, and the Midwest Poetry Review Prize. In Bombay she won the Bahut Tantrika Kamala Das Competition. Her first book, *A Spelling Guide to Woman,* was published in 1991. She is a practising student counsellor and family therapist.

Charmayne D'Souza, in a note on her writing says: 'The poet must write as if he had no brother nor sister, no cousin, aunt, uncle nor constitution. I'm tempted to say no country, but then I have always been accused of writing as if I did not have one. It's not that I have a sense of rootlessness or alienation, but I think I write about vivid inner experiences rather than of localized spaces. Maybe I will change as I become far-sighted with age.'

Charmayne D'Souza, who belongs to a younger generation of poets, feels, as other poets sometimes do, that poetry becomes increasingly difficult to write after one's first book. 'What will my students think? My in-laws? My husband?' Her first experience of writing was more like automatic writing. After the death of her father when she was 21, she 'just filled five hundred-page notebooks endlessly with nonsense rhymes'. Her first contact with other poets was at the home of Kamala Das where she was taken by Saleem Peeradina for a poetry reading session. 'I suddenly felt', she says, 'as if I had arrived at the right place.'

Some of Charmayne D'Souza's poems are about the situation of women. Others are about landscapes, visits to museums, prisoners, schools for the handicapped. Her talent is displayed at its best in poems such as 'The White Line Down the Road to Minnesota', when she contemplates an object and allows a number of images and ideas to arise from it without being whimsical or arbitrary. 'God's Will?' handles the idea of a tragic world with deft irony. 'Strange Bedfellows' enters an obsessively violent mind and ends with chilling finality. When the poems do not work it tends to be because ideas are overstated or punch lines fall flat. Fortunately, not too many poems fall into this category.

from *A Spelling Guide to Woman*

When God First Made a Whore

When God first made a whore,
He took the howl of the wolf,
the flexibility of the politician's
law,
and the smoothness of the guillotine's
saw.
Said the Almighty Lord:
'Men, I have given you
the Almighty Broad.'

She said — 'Look after me well,
for upon my body lie many sleepers,
converging into nothingness
like a railway track.
My body is the single straw
that shook once in the wind,
and finally broke the camel's back.
It will be the last life
left to the cat,
the sinking ship to a deserting
rat,
a barren cannon booming
in a fertile field of men,
a Rorschach test of loneliness
looming
like the celibate's final amen.
My body
is a coffin creak
and the tap-tap of a desolate
shutter,
it's the cuckold's last silent
shriek
and the village idiot's stutter.

Adam's rib
chewed to bone, to blood,

and the stone
that hurled Abel to the mud.

One day,
God will ask for this sweaty body
of mine,
but, like all the rest,
He will have to stand in line.

So said the whore,
as they asked for more.

The White Line
Down the Road to Minnesota

It wings down the road,
seagulling to its own path,
unidirectional —
little knowing what it achieves
in its whiteness,
dividing left from right,
those coming from those going,
those being overtaken
from those overtaking.

The white line
is not for the blind, then,
but only for those
who tread a certain borderline.

A pole star
for the city traveller,
a beaten track
for 55 m.p.h. riders,
a skunk stripe
for those escaping life,
a life-line for those moving on,
a strait-jacket
for those yet unborn.

I Would Like to Have
a Movie Cowboy for a Husband

A lean back,
walking into the sagebrush,
with infinite possibilities
of never returning again,
exterminated by an inscrutable
        Comanche,
a stubbled renegade,
or a crook general,
introducing — my husband.

Our lovemaking
would have the sweep
of brushfire,
our orgasms
the crisp certainty
of death,
our life
the aroma of fried bread, beans and hash,
and the guarantee,
always lurking somewhere
in the background,
that the goods would last for only
two or three years,
that our marriage could be
deliciously
wiped out,
like an Indian tribe,
forever.

Strange Bedfellows

I have marked this woman out
for me.
We will be tied together
by the scarlet sari
of her blood.

Seven times around
the fire of my shots.

What I have done
is done
for all my unborn sons.

Her mangalsutra
will be a bullet
to her breast,

My garland
a hempen rope
around my neck

and a swift sharp
erection
into death.

God's Will?

A strange legacy, that:
one holocaust,
thirty-five wars,
a few million tortured and killed.

Am I heir to all that?
Or did some crafty lawyer
put in a side-clause
I knew nothing about?

I understood:
my holdings were to consist
of one slice of good earth,
a dove bearing an olive branch,
a rainbow bowing to the sun,
and, of course,
my daily bread.

So far,
I have not received
any

of this movable or immovable
property.

I ask you:
is the will still valid?
Am I still an heir?

Our apologies, Sir, Madame,
for the delay,
but your quarrel is only
with the dead,
and we have reason to believe
that He whom you speak of
is still alive.

Judith

If I could,
I would cut off
my lovers' heads
one by one,
and serenade them
to sleep in my spare time.

Most are ghosts, anyway.
They have blissed
my imagination,
have not in any way
interfered with my life,
except in sleep.

Those that keep me awake
deserve their heads
on a pike,
and not on a pillow.
Where's my sword, I say?

Tara Patel

Born 1949. Tara Patel was educated in Gujarat and Malaysia. She is a freelance journalist and columnist. *Single Woman,* her first book, was published in 1992.

The predominant tone of Tara Patel's work is a weariness so extreme that at times it sounds almost posthumous. The weariness stems from relationships that don't work, a sense of being the odd person out when everyone else seems to be alright, the demands of city life.

In its own way, *Single Woman* is a brave book. It cannot have been easy to write poems in which the speakers express need so openly, unsheltered by irony. Feminist critics concerned with placing poets on a political spectrum would not necessarily approve.

On a poetry spectrum Tara Patel does rather better: 'Listening to my own confessions is a / third-degree past-time.' ('In a Working Women's Hostel'). 'A woman's life is a reaction / to the crack of a whip./ She learns to dodge it as it whistles / around her / but sometimes it lands on the thick, / distorted welt of her memory' ('Woman'). 'In Bombay' is probably her best poem, catching as it does the desolation of being unemployed. 'Unemployed, one makes friends who/are unemployed, / Picked up at the employment bureau / where silence is articulate. / The unemployed dare not lose their temper'. Patel's poems are haunting, in their rhythm, words and insight.

Nissim Ezekiel, who is in touch with the poet when she comes to Bombay, says that Tara Patel is convinced she is not a poet. Of course, as with all poets, she has poems that don't work, but her conclusion about herself is extreme. Perhaps it demonstrates an uncertainty of which only the genuine article is capable.

from *Single Woman*

Woman

A woman's life is a reaction
to the crack of a whip.
She learns to dodge it as it whistles
around her
but sometimes it lands on the thick,
distorted welt of her memory,
reminding her of lessons learned
in the past.
Then in rebellion she turned her face
to the whip,
till pain became a river in flood
wreaking vengeance.
She ran away to live as an escaped convict,
or a refugee,
or a yogi in the wilderness of civilization.
Beneath the thick, distorted welt of her memory,
she dreams,
anyone could have touched baby-smooth skin
with kisses.

Request

Sometimes for old times sake
you should look me up.
Have lunch with me, I'll pay the bill.
How little I know you though I loved
you for so long,
and still do for old times sake.

You cannot forget me so completely.
Remember me a little and meet me sometimes.
Once in a while, for good luck,
do not negate the past.
Indulge me.

Not because I want to embarrass you.
It is not your lack of love which distresses
me any more.
I'm no longer obsessed with a blind emotion
which promises everything and nothing.
You have to be young forever to be in love
like that.

I will not bore you with details of how I lived
for months after your exit.
But because I'm pining for an old pleasure,
have lunch with me one of these days.
I miss you most when I'm eating alone.

A man should look up a woman sometimes
for old times sake.
For reasons other than those which are obsolete.
Have lunch with me,
I'll pay the bill.

Calangute Beach, Goa

II
(For Howard)

After a two-day holiday,
not the doll-faced German —
Dresden china, aquamarine in his eyes,
but the American,
hangs as a pin-up in my mind.

When we met his 'Hello' was quick,
mine slow.
Coconut oil ripened colour on his body.
After lunch our conversation was too long.
Exchanging notes on East and West
I asked his name,
he didn't ask mine.

The matrimonial ads in the Indian newspapers
amused him.

His invitation to go swimming naked
was turned down.
A long brown look accentuated the loneliness
of my inhibitions.

Both of us knew,
there was no time for the persuasions
I needed.
I should have gone to share the sun's wine with him.
In such a man's arms it must be
permanently afternoon.

A goodbye can be a hug and
'Women's lib in India is skin-deep, baby.'
For weeks I can brood of nothing else.
He is a growing regret,
a red bulb off and on reminding me of men
I cannot afford.

In Bombay

Time passes even when unemployed.

After summer the incessant monologue of rain.
There is a professional touch to it all.
I have been employed as many times
as unemployed.
And now I am unemployed.
Repetition does not make it easier.

In the beginning one leaves the house
in the morning as usual.
Pretences increase, imaginary interviews
outnumber unimaginary ones.
Waiting to be interviewed is a
test by itself.

Unemployed, one makes friends who
are unemployed.
Picked up at the employment bureau
where silence is articulate.
The unemployed dare not lose their temper.

The afternoons are reserved for exhibitions,
libraries, bookstalls.
Movies. Today it was *Wait until Dark*
for the second time.
I am an outsider in an auditorium of
college students.

The boys are quick with gilded wit, the
girls gay dolls
with 'Choosy Cherry' lips and expensive eyes.
My white-washed presence marred the
illustration.

Of course, when unemployed, the need to spend,
to do everything in excess, increases.
Cursing comes easily, when a hundred-rupee
note is lost or stolen
it is God who is a so and so.

Unemployed people try to sleep at any
time of the day.

In a Working Women's Hostel

1

The evening is an experience of high tide.
I escape. Twelve storeys above the city
the terrace is my great outdoors.
Rs 350 p.m. to meet God is not much at all.
Somewhere along the skyscraper skyline
I walk to and fro. A nun without a vocation!

Am I lonely? Or am I a loner? The difference
must be resolved quickly now.
My private communion is overlooked by superior
balconies, terraces.
The sun makes a wedding finale. A henna-
coloured horizon, smudged eyeshadow clouds.

A patchwork of lights coming on compete
gaudily with the stars.

The rising full moon tells a familiar story.
A breeze purrs, inspires fear, I trip over
the silver wings fluttering on the crazy floor.
A distant sea roars in my ears.

Up here flight is a dangerous illusion.
Crying is a terminal argument. I
return to my room.

2

Waking up at night is a symptom of aging.
I kick aside the warm weather of my blanket,
the touch of my own thighs, breasts,
is an embarrassment.
In the winter cold I fold myself up in supplication
to hear myself more clearly.

Listening to my own confessions is a
third-degree past-time.
I function as a one-woman courtroom.
I have sealed up my life in black envelopes
addressed to no one in particular.
'Confidential. It is the rough wool of a man
you want tonight and every night.'

'A woman can feed herself. Love begins
with a man.'
And so on and so on. The colour of bones
is in my hair now
and I have come to a standstill.
The passing days have a posthumous
touch to them.

Index of First Lines

A lean back, 86
A man in love is in love with his
    own shadow, 66
A strange legacy, that: 87
A woman's life is a reaction 90
Adam, your namesake lives 55
After a two-day holiday, 91
After eight years of marriage 25
As we came out of the church
    43
At sunset, on the river bank,
    Krishna 13

Bird broken on a flying wing 36

Did you expect dignity? 51

Father, you will be proud to
    know 31
Fond husband, ancient settler
    in the mind, 16
For you M, I undid all my
    hopes. 34
Francis X D'Souza 39

Gently touch the earth. 34
Getting a man to love you is
    easy 15
Great Pan is not dead; 75

He holds out his lips, 76
Her hand sweeps over the
    rough grained paper, 77
His loud sharp call 73
How close we felt 22

I'd live you as a Saturday night
    memory 24

I cannot hold you in my hand
    for long 33
I don't know politics but I know
    the names 10
I have marked this woman out
    86
I lost this last bit of shine 33
I no longer feel I'm Mamta
    Kalia. 26
I want to pick my nose 21
I was born a foreigner. 58
If I could, 88
If I were to set stock 62
Impossible to hold, 55
In every Catholic home there's
    a picture 43
It's time to find a place 47
It drifts slowly, dreaming. This
    is 63
It was only in sleep that he 13
It wings down the road, 85

Let us forget your death and
    mine. 25
Looking at my navel 24
Love-lorn, 12
Lying in bed on a pure-white
    sheet, the 67

M. assures me she'll be back
    44
Making sure there's no one
    around 63
My eyes lick them off the page;
    65

Near the sea behind Cadell
    Road 14

INDEX OF FIRST LINES

Once you thought it good 40
One day they said 50

Right, now here it comes. 41

She dreamt of descending 39
She sits on the rattan chair, 67
So many things 21
Sometimes for old times sake
    90
Sometimes the nine-year-old
    boy 79
Sudden impact. 57

Tall hill speckled with pine; 65
The bolt bangs in. 56
The calendar has just dropped
    22
The evening is an experience of
    high tide. 93
The guests have departed. 64
The hills crawl with convoys. 42
The sea receded. The dunes
    remember. 46
The way I returned again and

again to your self-portrait
    with blue irises 74
The women of Leh are such —
    75
There are just not enough 54
Things were meant to flow 53
This station has no name. 29
Time passes even when un-
    employed. 92
Twenty years ago 29

We have spent our youth in
    gentle sinning 11
When a man is dead, or a
    woman, 12
When God first made a whore,
    84
Who cares for you, Papa? 20
Who speaks of the strong cur-
    rents 78

You curl into your mouth. 35
You hold the toy at me 30
You planned to tame a swallow,
    to hold her 15